Syrian Refugees and Agriculture in Turkey

Syrian Refugees and Agriculture in Turkey

Work, Precarity and Survival

Saniye Dedeoglu

I.B. TAURIS
LONDON • NEW YORK • OXFORD • NEW DELHI • SYDNEY

I.B. TAURIS
Bloomsbury Publishing Plc
50 Bedford Square, London, WC1B 3DP, UK
1385 Broadway, New York, NY 10018, USA
29 Earlsfort Terrace, Dublin 2, Ireland

BLOOMSBURY, I.B. TAURIS and the I.B. Tauris logo are trademarks of Bloomsbury Publishing Plc

First published in Great Britain 2022
This paperback edition published 2023

Copyright © Saniye Dedeoglu, 2022

Saniye Dedeoglu has asserted her right under the Copyright, Designs and Patents Act, 1988, to be identified as Author of this work.

For legal purposes the Acknowledgements on p. xi constitute an extension of this copyright page.

Cover image © Kurtuluş Karaşin, Development Workshop, Adana, 2016

All rights reserved. No part of this publication may be reproduced or transmitted in any form or by any means, electronic or mechanical, including photocopying, recording, or any information storage or retrieval system, without prior permission in writing from the publishers.

Bloomsbury Publishing Plc does not have any control over, or responsibility for, any third-party websites referred to or in this book. All internet addresses given in this book were correct at the time of going to press. The author and publisher regret any inconvenience caused if addresses have changed or sites have ceased to exist, but can accept no responsibility for any such changes.

A catalogue record for this book is available from the British Library.

A catalog record for this book is available from the Library of Congress.

ISBN: HB: 978-0-7556-3448-4
PB: 978-0-7556-4654-8
ePDF: 978-0-7556-3449-1
eBook: 978-0-7556-3405-7

Typeset by Deanta Global Publishing Services, Chennai, India

To find out more about our authors and books visit www.bloomsbury.com and sign up for our newsletters.

To my beloved Ayşe Defne

Contents

List of Illustrations	viii
Preface	ix
Acknowledgements	xi
1 Introduction	1
2 Precarization, intersecting vulnerabilities and work regimes: A context-specific theorization	15
3 Bitter lives on fertile lands: Seasonal agricultural work and migrant labour in Turkey	29
4 Syrians in Turkey: From guests to refugees	49
5 Intersecting vulnerabilities of the labour supply: Syrian women and children	65
6 Bonded labour: Recruitment, remuneration and retention	103
7 Conclusion	133
Notes	145
Bibliography	149
Index	162

Illustrations

Figures

3.1	Turkey's map of cash crops and demand for seasonal agricultural workers	37
3.2	Seasonal agricultural tent settlement in Adana	40
3.3	A group of seasonal agricultural workers at work	42
4.1	A group of Syrian workers planting cauliflower in Adana	61
5.1	Agriculture work by gender and age groups	67
5.2	A group of women workers in Adana	70
5.3	Syrian women workers in Adana's fields	72
5.4	A woman cooking for her children near her tent	77
5.5	Syrian women's marital statues and employment	81
5.6	Children packing onions	88
5.7	A boy picking cotton with his mother	94
5.8	A group of workers in a field	99
6.1	A sample of a wage card	121
6.2	A worker camp site	125
6.3	Inside a tent and food preparation	127
6.4	Young children having a nap in a tent	128

Tables

6.1	Sources of Labour for Recruitment in Adana	112
6.2	Methods for Worker Recruitment	114

Preface

The research I undertook for this book had started long ago before it came into life, and it has opened a new window for me to understand the life-worlds of seasonal agricultural workers in Turkey. Without a doubt this is an unjust and unequal world full of contradictions and conflicts. In this chaos and inequalities, labour seems to be the only medium to comprehend the lives and survival of many families trying to make a living at the edge of global economies. As a researcher, I have always aimed to bring out women's voices and views by using the research tools provided by interdisciplinary fields, such as gender and migration studies. This pursuit has also tended to centre on women's work practices and gender relations, which shape the very nature of the practice of earning a living. This time, my projection was not only on Syrian women but also on Syrian agricultural worker families and children.

Having this vantage point has also enabled me to analyse not only the life-worlds of women but also the ways in which women shape the political, social, cultural and economic changes taking place in the societies in which they live. Thus, it is always important to understand not only the socio-economic transformations through the lenses of gender and migration studies but also the role women play in these grand transformations. That is why this book chooses to focus on one segment of economic life, that is agricultural work, in which women seem to be quite invisible, with an aim to unleash the gendered aspect of habitus, even in the least expected areas.

Together with the arrival of a large number of Syrians, Turkey is home to the largest Syrian refugee community in the world and the agricultural sector offers work opportunities for vulnerable Syrian refugee families. This book exposes the fast-changing relationship between seasonal agricultural production and the work practices of Syrian refugees in Turkey. Through close ethnographic study I carried out over four years with nearly 1,000 people, the book illuminates how the increasing number of incoming Syrians results in the 'precarization' of the workers – particularly women and children. I examine Syrian families' working and living conditions with a special interest in the dynamics of how they utilize the labour of women and children to survive and have access to work.

I conducted an in-depth study of the Syrian community – at a time when the state apparatus is hostile to research on the subject; the material in this book is unique and offers an insight into remote agricultural sites that are invisible to many. It is an analysis of the precarization process of Syrian labour in an industry that wants to attract the most vulnerable people into the workforce. By focusing on the intersectional vulnerabilities and the context-dependent precarization, the book argues that the commercialization of agricultural production and the increasing use of waged labour bloom antagonistic encounters of different ethnic, cultural and religious groups in rural Turkey.

Acknowledgements

The book is the result of a string of research and fieldwork I undertook between 2015 and 2019 to examine the lives of seasonal agricultural workers in different parts of Turkey. In this endeavour, I worked with different institutions and people, but among others, the Development Workshop (DW) Cooperative has been the home of that string of research. I thank DW and its team for allowing me to observe the living and working experiences of seasonal agricultural workers and to go after the questions I sought to answer. I also thank Kurtuluş Karaşin for sharing his photo to be the cover image of the book.

My special thanks also go to Aslı Şahankaya for being with me in each and every step of the way. I thank my colleagues at the University of Mugla – Ummuhan Gökoavlı, Çisel Ekiz Gökmen, Aysun Danışman and Bilge Şentürk – for making life bearable and lighting it in the difficult times of the Covid-19 pandemic and of the writing process. Solidarity endures in unusual ways. My family has always provided me with unlimited support, and it would not have been possible for me to write this book without their support and guidance. My daughter has been the cheerer when I needed a little boost to go on with the writing. My utmost appreciation goes to all these people.

Finally, to the seasonal agricultural worker families who generously opened up their homes and hearts to me. No words of thanks are enough. I only hope that I have managed to remain somewhat true to their perspectives and stories, and that these perspectives will find their way into broader debates about the issues of refugees, gender and social integration in Turkey and strategies for advancing women's and children's interests in general.

1

Introduction

This study is an account of Syrian refugees' involvement in seasonal agricultural work in Turkey, a site of precarization of labour markets, and specifically women's and children's central role in a work regime that continuously seeks paths towards bonded labour. It explores the relationship between labour supply and demand in Turkey's seasonal agricultural labour markets, which are continuously geared towards tapping into the most vulnerable sources of the labour pool to reduce production costs. The book seeks mainly to answer the question: 'under what conditions does precarization occur for workers in Turkey's agricultural labour?' It also follows the ways of how women's and children's labour has played a central role in the precarization of Syrians in a work regime that continuously seeks paths to bond labour. The material illuminates the strategies and responses of both the poorest labour segment (Syrian refugees) and other actors, especially labour intermediaries (*dayıbaşı* or *elci* in Turkish). It also explores the strategies employed in agricultural production in general and examines the contribution of migrant labour to the competitive strength of the Turkish seasonal agricultural sector in global food markets.

Sharing the basic premise of Castels's analysis of migratory processes in *International Human Mobility: Key Issues and Challenges to Social Theory* (2015), which are shaped by both macro-social structures and the actions and perceptions of affected populations, migrants and non-migrants, I argue that global agricultural production relies increasingly on strategies that attract diversified forms of labour with intersecting vulnerabilities and on the adaptation of labour control practices that generate a form of bonded labour. The concerted efforts of the actors involved in seasonal agricultural production in Turkey to find and retain cheap sources of labour exploit Syrian workers, and Syrian refugees also hold onto their precarious agricultural jobs by integrating the most vulnerable members of their families into the workforce, that is, women and children.

Various studies have depicted migrant labour as instrumental in increasing the precarization of the labour force worldwide. The extreme forms of labour exploitation experienced by migrant workers, labelled as 'hyper-precarity', play a central role in the precarization of employment (Lewis et al., 2015). Many studies have emphasized the instabilities and insecurities particular vulnerable groups – such as migrants, refugees and asylum seekers – experience in employment and workplaces, documenting how they can be compelled, coerced or restricted into highly exploitative work (e.g. Jordan and Brown, 2007; Lewis et al., 2015). Migrants' 'life-worlds . . . are inflected with uncertainty and instability' (Waite, 2009: 416), which increase their representation in the 'migrant precariat' (Schierup et al., 2014; Schierup et al., 2015). Migrant workers are engaged in precarious work around the globe, but their experiences differ in complex, but socially patterned, ways.

The precarization of labour all over the world goes hand in hand with increasing transnational migratory movements that are partially the result of rising demands for casual labour in many sectors following global economic restructuring. Many production sites in urban, but also in rural, Turkey have experienced a similar trend of a growing demand for migrant labour. Agriculture in Turkey has been one of the major sectors with high demand for migrant workers as its need for waged workers has been increasing steadily since the early 1990s. With the arrival of Syrian refugees since 2011, when internal conflict erupted in Syria, refugee labour in seasonal agricultural work in Turkey has grown significantly. Syrians work mainly in seasonal agricultural production in which workers travel to different provinces to undertake employment during high seasons of a given product.

As shown by Martin Bak Jørgensen (2016), precarization as a string of procedural aspects is context dependent and may take different forms in different socio-economic settings. The empirical sections of my work document how context-dependent strategies absorb and generate precarious workers, in particular Syrian refugees in Turkey's seasonal agricultural sector, an industry producing for world markets. The precarization of Syrian labour is generated through a set of strategies applied in the agricultural sector integrating the most vulnerable labour force (women and children) and the sector's labour demand strategies (recruitment, retention and remuneration [3Rs], using such methods as labour intermediaries, secluded refugee settlements and a specific wage payment system). By focusing on intersectional vulnerabilities and context-dependent precarization in exploring the labour market integration of Syrian refugees, the book shows that differential inclusion of migrant labour through gender, ethnicity, age and patriarchal relations supports the precarization of Syrian labour by increasing the bargaining power of migrant labour, namely the domestic native Turkish precariat. The book, therefore, contributes to the literature on migration and labour studies, as well as female and child migrant labour. It draws on anthropological and sociological perspectives to address questions of critical importance to the social sciences.

Research was conducted among the Syrian workers of Turkey's seasonal agricultural sector, an important sector for its capacity, not only to export worldwide but also to supply cheap products for domestic consumption. I have collected rich empirical data that provides analysis of who exactly works, under what conditions they work and how they interact with other local groups. At a descriptive level, the book reveals the lives of Syrian refugees in the insecure, invisible and low/unpaid end of the labour market and the labour relations of a quite peculiar production – seasonal agricultural work – and its place in national and global markets.

The objectives of the book

My study has three objectives. The first objective is to explore the nature of Syrian refugees' work and help render it visible in Turkey's seasonal agricultural labour markets, where most of the work takes place informally. Turkey is home to the largest Syrian refugee community in the world, and the overwhelming majority of refugees live outside refugee camps and struggle to make a living. Agriculture offers a wide range of work opportunities for vulnerable Syrian workers, and the host country's landlords and agricultural labour brokers have welcomed Syrian refugee families whose involvement helps to reduce average wages in seasonal agricultural work in many parts of Turkey. Literature concerned with migrant work in seasonal agricultural production typically focuses on Western countries, where most workers are temporary migrants who move across countries seasonally. Syrians in Turkey, in contrast, are permanent workers who are changing the very nature of seasonal agricultural work in Turkey.

With a focus on the precarization of Syrian labour in Turkish seasonal agricultural work, my second objective is to examine the supply factors that condition Syrians' work. As of August 2020, the Syrian population in Turkey has exceeded 3.5 million and is composed mostly of young people under the age of eighteen and women with low educational attainment. Many have settled in large cities, such as Istanbul, İzmir and Bursa, where employment opportunities are more diverse than in smaller locales, but the majority remain in cities near the Syrian border, such as Hayat, Kilis, Şanlıurfa and Gaziantep. Syrians have emerged as a new precariat of the Turkish economy.

The sudden arrival of Syrian refugees has presented a new dynamic in the most labour-intensive, often informal sectors, such as textiles, tourism, construction and agriculture: competition for the most precarious jobs among the poor – the precariat. Syrians have been taking a lion's share of most casual jobs in the agricultural sector. Integration of the most disadvantaged groups into the labour force in recent years has intensified the precarization of the labour force and has generated competition among different worker groups for existing jobs. The integration of Syrians into agricultural work is largely based on a string of absorption strategies adopted both by refugees competing to access these jobs – supply-side strategies – and by the sector seeking to integrate the most vulnerable labour force. The supply-side strategies of Syrian refugees have been constructed to win the rivalry between poverty-stricken groups and have resulted in the deployment of the most vulnerable segments of the Syrian population, namely, women and children. An infinite capacity to control female and child labour is an important aspect of the seasonal agricultural labour market, and control over workers takes many shapes, handed over from the heads of households to labour intermediaries and then to landowner employers.

The winning strategy of Syrian refugees in this competition is to tap into the large labour pool of women and children, whose labour is essential for production in the fields and also enables social reproduction of worker families. Moreover, the book dwells on the concept of 'differential inclusion' (Mezzadra and Nielsen, 2013: 165), which refers to the role of the border in selecting, filtering and differentiating migrant labour and to the inclusion of different kinds of migrants, from different levels of subordination that shape labour markets and intersectional vulnerabilities, as forms of embodiments of interconnected disadvantages based on social categorizations, such as race, ethnicity, class, gender and social status (e.g. being migrants). The concept of 'vulnerable integration' refers to the inclusion of the most vulnerable segments of migrant labour in the face of this competition. By adopting Polanyi's concept of 'double movement',[1] as an agency through which people develop varying forms of agency and resistance, my objective is to analyse how female and child labour are used in seasonal agricultural work and why refugee families have increasingly relied on these two categories of labour to gain access to agricultural jobs. This analysis enables to form the fact that the interactions of structure and agency are an integral part of social transformations but, in return, affect how global social transformations played out on national, local, household and individual levels. The book traces the impact of global capitalism on refugees and their households and focuses on social transformations steering antagonistic confrontations between different ethnic, religious and cultural groups in rural Turkey. In this setting, the agency of refugees is limited not only to their potential of earning a living and supporting their families but also to their strategies to manage the confrontations and rivalry existing in Turkey's agricultural sector.

My third objective is to provide an understanding of the labour demand strategies conditioning Syrian refugees' entry into agricultural wage work in Turkey. Isolated tent settlements (retention), labour intermediaries (recruitment) and a specific type of wage payment system (remuneration) are distinctive strategies the sector has adopted to organize its labour process. The 3R strategies reveal the broader interrelated structural process in which both structure and agency play a crucial role in reproducing, challenging and reconstructing the power relations in the labour market. The use of migrant labour in agricultural production illustrates the transnational connectedness that affects national societies, local communities and individuals (Castels, 2015). The result of the adoption of these strategies is that migrant workers are more vulnerable, more flexible and more competitive and therefore more attractive in meeting the demands of the sector seeking cheaper labour.

In an overall assessment, my main argument is that the influx of Syrian refugees has led to the further precarization of agricultural labour in Turkey since Syrian agricultural worker families practice family-based work arrangements in which fathers/husbands wield patriarchal control more aggressively over women and children who disproportionally work in seasonal harvesting cycles. This feminization of Turkey's agricultural labour – the increasing reliance on the work of female and child Syrian refugees who receive lower wages and accept harsher worker conditions – has led to its precarization. Moreover, Syrian refugees mostly do not possess formal work papers and thus are considered 'irregular' migrants whose basic wages are not guaranteed in the agricultural sector. Due to high housing costs, they often accept company-provided housing and other services from Turkish farmers, who trap them in 'bonded' labour relations in which it is difficult for them to escape.

My argument in the book shows how Syrian female and child labour are used in paid and unpaid activities directly related to the production of low-cost crops that compete in international markets or support low wages of domestic consumers. The intersecting vulnerabilities of female and child labour whose labour has been a part of successful negotiation process of Syrians enable further precarization of agricultural labour in Turkey. Moving all members of a family together to work is the strongest indication of how worker families rely on the interconnectedness of productive and reproductive work to gain access to income-earning potential in the agricultural sector, mostly through immeasurable use of female labour. Productive work in agriculture is only possible because of the work women perform in the realm of reproductive work, which systematically subsidizes capital and enables ultra-exploitation of migrant labour. Therefore, an analysis of the precarization of refugee labour is considerably determined not only under the impact of intensification and/or informalization of productive work but also in the ways social reproduction internalizes production costs to workers, families and communities, in this case Syrians.

On another level, the book argues that the precarization of Syrian labour is not only affected by the living arrangements but also by the recruitment of the agricultural labour force, organization into working teams and transportation to the fields. This research will help to show that labour markets are bearers of social relations, in the sense that they are instantiations of the social, ethnic and gender relations in the society in which the labour market is embedded. Social relations as bearers of class, ethnic and gender relations reflect existing problems of social domination and subordination at institutional levels, such as household, community, the market and the state. Embeddedness of the labour market in Turkey results in the invisibility of migrant workers in agriculture without any public recognition of the work that is done, even in the case where the contribution workers make has a great deal of importance for their families, their communities, their country and world production. This book contributes to studying how the world of labour markets is being transformed through a bottom-up process as a result of the economic activities of migrants and their distinctive ways of social integration – vulnerable integration – into their host society.

Research methodology

Migration research is historically motivated by the need to measure and control migrant labour in a colonial or post-colonial context. Thus, its focus has been on 'male labour migration', the central concern of policymakers. Until very recently, women were mostly invisible, due to normative assumptions that they either were totally absent from the migration process or were present as passive 'family members' of male migrant workers. The most gender-neutral research explicitly reflects men's experience. In the rare cases where women's presence is acknowledged, their contribution to the economic and social realities of the host country is often ignored or underestimated (Kofman et al., 2000: 3). When women are portrayed, they are often pictured as 'backward-looking . . . guardians of family unity and the culture of origin' (Council of Europe, 1995: 32). Metso and Le Feuvre (2006) show that some large statistical data is composed of genderless migrants. It is only when estimating levels of human trafficking that the statistics present a gendered perspective, thus making women appear exclusively the passive victims of forced migration for domestic servitude or sexual exploitation.

Feminist methodology is therefore important to use in further developing women's experiences of migration from different angles. As Marjorie DeVault (1996) states, 'Feminist methodology provides the outline for a possible alternative to the distanced, distorting and dispassionately objective producers of much social research' (1996:34). Feminist methodology is designed to shift the focus of standard research from men's concerns to women's concerns. It employs methods that minimize harm and control in the research process and supports research of value to women, leading to social change or action beneficial to women (DeVault, 1996:32). This methodology uses mostly qualitative research tools which are often thought to value subjective and personal meanings, and it is said to be conducive to giving a voice to the most oppressed groups in society, while quantitative research is constructed in terms of testing theories and making predictions in an objective and value-free way (Metso and Le Feuvre, 2006).

Chamberlayne and Rustin note that a biographical approach, by contextualizing statistical data and demonstrating what they mean for individual lives, contains implications for social policy, and furthermore that such an approach can highlight the network of existing relations between the individual and others (1999:21). Lummis (1987) discusses the use of individual biographies and their connections with the structure and social relations.

> The point is that people live their lives within the material and cultural boundaries of their time span, and so life histories are exceptionally effective historical sources because through the totality of lived experience they reveal relations between individuals and social forces, which are rarely apparent in other sources. (Lummis, 1987:107–8)

I have also found that a qualitative and biographical approach is the most appropriate in exploring women's integration into the Turkish labour force. I use in-depth interviews with open-ended and non-structured questions. I also collected oral narratives to give voice to my subjects, especially Syrian women whose experiences as seasonal agricultural workers are at the centre of this study. This method is the most suitable way to describe and analyse migrants and migrant women's experiences from their own perspectives. This approach also captures interactions and interconnections between people and events, as they provide flexibility for explanation and allow space for narrators to express themselves by reducing the control and direction of the interviewer over the interviewee (Borland, 1991; Gluck and Patai, 1991). In addition, open-ended and in-depth interviews, according to Anderson and Jack, represent a shift from asking the right questions to focusing on the process and 'the dynamic unfolding nature of the subject's viewpoint' (1991:23).

The book is based on lengthy fieldwork in remote agricultural sites, invisible to many, not only researchers but also ordinary people. I have spent more than four years researching seasonal agricultural workers and have visited their living and working environments on a number of occasions between 2015 and

2019. During my first research trip, in 2015, I explored the role of migrant labour in Turkey's agricultural production, visited more than 10 rural provinces and interviewed 110 people. This research covered almost all major crops Turkey produced, ranging from hazelnuts, tea leaves, cotton, vegetables and many kinds of fruits. Three major migrant groups – Azerbaijanis, Georgians and Syrians – worked in agricultural production at the time. The interviews focused on migrants' journeys, living conditions, access to education and health care, work experience as agricultural workers and future prospects.

After collecting quantitative data in 2015, I collected qualitative data on Syrians in Adana in 2017.[2] I collected information on 905 people, using a questionnaire designed to include both open-ended and multiple-choice answers questions, conducted by a survey team in Arabic, of 112 worker households selected within the tent settlements in the four districts of Adana: Yüreğir, Seyhan, Karataş and Yumurtalık.[3] I selected the province of Adana because it hosts a large number of agricultural workers and boasts large-scale agricultural landholdings that generate a high demand for waged agricultural labourers. In Adana, agricultural production takes place throughout the year since it is one of the most fertile agricultural lands of Turkey, producing a vast range of products, predominantly cotton and all types of vegetables and fruits. The selection of the Adana Plain as a research site enabled an understanding of the dynamics in the labour market and the strategies that Syrians use to replace a large segment of the domestic labour force and put intersectional vulnerabilities into play to bargain for jobs.

The sample of 905 people was distributed equally between men and women, and almost half (45.2 per cent) were under the age of 18.[4] Due to the young age composition and mostly rural background of Syrian agricultural workers, the educational attainment was extremely low. Almost half of the population (47 per cent) was illiterate, and primary school graduates made up only 22.5 per cent. Dropouts from primary school (9.8 per cent) and secondary education (4.6 per cent) were also high. More than half (53.6 per cent) of the sample were agricultural workers back in Syria and 18.8 per cent were farmers. The questions aimed to understand Syrian household structure, legal status in Turkey, economic resources and working practices. Since no nationwide macro data were available on Syrian households, the data collected proved to be an important source of information on Syrian agricultural worker households, demographic composition and economic survival strategies. The data reveal distinctive characteristics of Syrian households: the average length of stay was 3.5 years, a typical household was composed of eight people, and 80 per cent of all families were from Halep and Haseke. All of the families had stayed in refugee camps, and 17 per cent were not registered with Turkish authorities and had no identification cards.

This stream of data collection also included in-depth interviews with a total of fifty people, including twenty-five Syrian refugees, ten local workers employed in agricultural work, ten landowners and five agricultural labour intermediaries – called a *dayıbaşı* or *elçi* locally (Pelek, 2010 and 2019). The respondents were selected among the questionnaire sample and weighted equally between women and men. Questions were relatively open-ended, designed to enable respondents to tell their stories in their own words. Lasted around forty-five minutes to one hour, interviews focused on their migration journeys, experiences before migrating to Turkey, experiences in Turkey (arrival, settlement and relationship with the natives), links with Syria and near-future plans. I used qualitative content analysis to identify a set of common themes from the narratives and then employed a thematic coding system with NVivo, which helped to create analytical categories. A thematic coding reflects the dimensions of integration, such as legal–political and socio-economic ones, which include experiences of accessing housing, employment, health and education, citizenship and social relations. I gained ethical approval for the project via the university's ethics committee and consent forms, which were circulated to participants before starting the interview process. I also assigned pseudonyms to the participants to ensure anonymity.

Through the book I use the terms 'migrants' and 'refugees' interchangeably when referring to Syrians in Turkey. However, they are indeed different terms. IOM (The International Organization for Migration) defines migrants as an umbrella term, not defined under international law, reflecting the common understanding of a person who moves away from his or her place of usual residence, whether within a country or across an international border, temporarily or permanently, and for a variety of reasons.[5] Refugee is a person who, owing to a well-founded fear of persecution for reasons of race, religion, nationality, membership of a particular social group or political opinion, is outside the country of his/her nationality and is unable or, owing to such fear, is unwilling to avail himself/herself of the protection of that country; or who, not having a nationality and being outside the country of his/her former habitual residence as a result of such events, is unable or, owing to such fear, is unwilling to return to it (IOM, 2019).

The selection of examples in the book was guided by my research 'objectives'. The book does not offer an exhaustive account of Syrians' lives but focuses on the economic and social strategies that are deployed and the 'cultures of solidarity' in response to the problem of their survival in a new home country (Fantasia, 1988:14). The data presented explores how Syrian workers attempt to not only maintain but also improve their lives.

Organization of the book

The structure and content of the book is designed to analyse the precarisation of migrant labour and the situation of Syrian seasonal workers in Turkey's agricultural sector. I begin in Chapter 2 by laying out the theory behind my work. The chapter illustrates how context-specific precarization may be a way of unveiling the interrelations between production and social reproduction, together with an analysis of the feminization of precarization in global agricultural production, in the context of wider debates concerning intersectionality, the precarization of life-worlds and the exploitation of labour. The chapter explains both the precarization of migrant labour in the southern counties in the twenty-first century and the integration of migration labour into existent work regimes that affect commercial agricultural production. It also includes an account of the intersecting vulnerabilities refugee women experience in the labour markets of their host countries as well as the interwoven relations between production and social reproduction in the contemporary capitalism which relies more and more on women's social reproductive labour to extract surplus value. The contention of this chapter is to show that the precarization of labour is extended beyond the relations governing labour relations in the realm of production to include social reproduction into labour relations as well as is shaped by the structure of work regimes that gear to keep labour bonded.

Chapter 3 outlines the macro-economic and social changes taking place in Turkey's agricultural sector and their implications for seasonal agricultural work and immigrants' employment in agricultural production. The presence of immigrant labour, Azerbaijani, Georgian and Syrian, in seasonal agricultural work has been the emergent phenomenon of restructuring in the agricultural sector, with female and child labour a particularly significant feature of seasonal farm work. They are, in fact, the main dynamics underlying the organization of seasonal agricultural work in Turkey.

Chapter 4 focuses on Syrian refugees in Turkey: their demographic characteristics, their legal status and precarization of their labour in Turkey's highly informal labour markets. The situation of Syrians in Turkey is a pendulum in which Syrians are, on the one hand, granted rights to stay in Turkey and have access to basic rights, with a formal path to integration, but on the other hand, they have quite limited access to formal work opportunities, leading to their informal integration into the labour market. This analysis contextualizes how the conflict between the legal and actual status of Syrians underlies their precarization in rural Turkey, as well as their working and living conditions.

The next two chapters deal with empirical material related to factors conditioning Syrian refugee labour in Turkey's agricultural sector. Chapter 5 focuses on women and children as the agents of precarization of Syrians whose labour is also at the crossroads of production and social reproduction on which the essence of seasonal agricultural work is based. The chapter opens with a discussion of the debate over the relatedness between production and social reproduction, which functions under the auspice of patriarchal and capitalist exploitative relations. The empirical sections conducted with a sample of Syrian worker households explore the role of women and children in ensuring the survival of their families and demonstrate that gender is an underlying concept to understand the nature of precarization and labour exploitation. Chapter 5 continues with the exploration of the centrality of child labour in seasonal farm work. Child labour is justified by families, labour intermediaries and farmers. By and large, the chapter shows that children's work in agriculture is instrumental for families in obtaining precarious jobs and for farmers in tapping into cheap labour forms. Syrian child workers have fewer opportunities than other children in education and few alternatives available to them to break free from hard agricultural labour. They are in a destitute situation as the new and youngest precariat of Turkey.

Chapter 6 develops the structures through which the seasonal agricultural labour market bonds workers: recruitment, retention and remuneration, or the 3Rs. The 3Rs are focused on concentrating labour in isolated tent camps, retaining workers' wages and using labour intermediaries. The 3Rs are the foundation of a bonded labour regime that allows access to cheap labour without a longer-term build-up of labour institutions that would lead to better working conditions and labour solidarities. The empirical findings examine how the role of labour intermediaries cuts across the areas of recruitment, remuneration and retention of workers and how these processes are acted out and sustained in Syrians' everyday lives. The 3Rs are reshaping the precarization of labour and the notion of embeddedness of labour markets in Turkey's seasonal agricultural work.

The final chapter summarizes the arguments and themes developed in the main body of the book. Some general conclusions are drawn from the research, concerning the degree of the precarization of labour in commercial agricultural production to assist in improving the conditions of seasonal agricultural workers, especially Syrian refugees in Turkey. The implications surrounding the changing nature of labour relations, commercial agriculture and migrant work in migrant hosting countries of the Global South are discussed to develop a context-specific analysis of the conditions of Syrian migrants living and working in rural Turkey. The chapter argues for a relational and perceptual understanding of the relationship between the precarization of labour and migration and its effects on local communities that encompasses the lifestyles and cultural practices of the communities in which the production takes place. From this perspective, the feminization of precarization and life-worlds of refugees are experienced as a result of competition with domestic workers to grab the most precarious jobs, while it is also enacted in a work regime that continuously strikes to bond labour through a number of strategies of the 3R regime of organization of seasonal agricultural labour markets in Turkey. The chapter closes by highlighting some important methodological issues that the research raises and points towards a new direction in migration, gender and work research agenda.

2

Precarization, intersecting vulnerabilities and work regimes

A context-specific theorization

Syrians have developed their own methods of obtaining informal agricultural jobs in rural Turkey through precarization, intersectional vulnerabilities and bonded labour. A context-specific analysis of precarization may help unveil the self-inflicted strategies migrants adopt to reach for jobs provided in a labour market that constantly seeks ways to exploit and bond their labour. Very broadly, precarization refers to the deteriorating job characteristics – such as low wages, low levels of protection and limited control over working hours and conditions and an increase in non-standard jobs worldwide – and the unstable forms of employment and life that condition the fact of being precariously treated as a particular characteristic of the current economy. While the debate on the political power of the precariat stems from Polanyi's theory of 'the double movement' (Polanyi, 2001), the precarization of migrant labour can be self-inflicted in the process of the 'race to the bottom' and competition among the poor in a haste for survival. In this regard, 'the double movement' of Syrian refugees is not a political act but a collection of strategies to eliminate rivals in the Turkish seasonal agricultural labour markets.

This chapter rests upon three distinct areas of precarization, and intersecting vulnerabilities and work regimes – bonded labour – analyses their relationships with each other through the lens of refugee women and children. The chapter sets the theoretical basis of a context-specific precarization of Syrian refugees in Turkey and focuses on the interconnectedness between the realms of production and social reproduction. By examining the concept of work regimes and bonded labour, the chapter pats how precarization is played out in a structure and macro-setting.

A key contention of this chapter is that gender is a facilitator of the precarization of migrant labour through its role in the realms of production and social reproduction. This chapter analyses the emerging issues in the gendering of the precarization of refugee labour and explores wider debates concerning the increasing significance of the intersectional vulnerabilities built upon the labour of women and children in refugee-hosting countries.

Precarization, feminization of precarity and social reproduction

The debate over precarization and migrant labour is underlined by the theme of hyper-exploitation and insecurities experienced by migrants. The emphasis on precarization has shifted slightly over time, from labour market conditions to the life-world of contemporary capitalism, and then to the identity of a class of workers; recent debates often focus on the politics of precarity by shifting the question from what precarity is to what precarity does and how precarious labour and precarious life intersect in particular times and places. This part of the chapter focuses on the concept of precarization and the relation established in the literature between feminization of precarity and the realm of social reproduction in which women are brought to the front of precarization not only through their labour in productive realm but also in social reproductive realm.

Precarity, precarization and migrant labour

Precarity commonly refers to marginal and casualized or contingent work. Although mostly associated with post-industrial societies of Western Europe and North America (Ettlinger, 2007; Waite, 2009), it has become a global phenomenon in recent decades and has extended to many different jobs and branches of an economy. The term is often viewed as a *condition* generated within specific labour markets, resulting in insecure and unstable work experiences (Arnold and Bongiovi, 2013; Fantone, 2007). Branch and Hanley (2011: 569) describe such work as 'uncertain, unpredictable, and risky from the point of view of the worker'. Specifically, some researchers view precarity as stemming from experiences of exploitation that primarily occur through the medium of time (period in a job, length of workday and shift patterns) (Anderson, 2007) and through processes of production (hiring practices, informality) that Tsianos and Papadopoulos (2006) emphasize as 'exploiting the continuum of everyday life'. Such labour markets, mainly in advanced capitalist economies, are said to be producing ever more precarious work (casual, short term and illegal), which is characterized by instability, lack of protection and social or economic vulnerability (see Waite, 2009: 416).

However, according to some analysts, precarity is 'the constitutive element of the new global disorder[,] to which [it] is very functional' (Schierup et al., 2014:50). A surplus population generated in this specific historical–structural context, reaching multiple millions, is at the disposal of transnational corporations, sub-contractors and franchises as a global reserve army (Schierup et al., 2014). Viewed thus not as a regrettable 'mistake', on the contrary, the excluded population are 'valuable' because they are 'vulnerable', and thus particularly exploitable (Bauder, 2006: 26). Precarity is also conceptualized as the process of 'expulsion' used by Saskia Sassen (2014: 1) for 'capturing the pathologies of today's global capitalism'. This understanding of precarity emphasizes a generalized condition of vulnerable populations not only by labour regimes but also and mainly by structural workings of global capitalism that often permeate the lives of many workers, including migrants and refugees. My purpose is to extend accounts of precarity beyond specific understandings of labour regimes and to recognize both the conditions and ambiguities of precarity in the migration context, specifically for Syrian agricultural workers in Turkey.

The term 'precariat', along with related terms, is important for understanding the work of Syrian refugees in Turkish agriculture. 'Precarious' refers to unstable forms of employment and life. 'Precarity' is 'a broader term for the condition of being precariously treated as a particular characteristic of the current economy'. 'Precariat' is a designation for 'people who live or work precariously'. And 'precariousness' refers to 'a broader sense of existential vulnerability' (Robinson, 2011).

According to Campbell and Price (2016), precariousness spans at least five different levels of social life: *precariousness in employment* refers to job characteristics, such as low wages, low levels of protection and limited control over working hours and conditions; *precarious work* often refers to non-standard, 'bad' jobs; *precarious workers* endure both the conditions and consequences of precariousness; *the precariat* is a virtual class of individuals sharing social and political attributes; and *precarity* refers to broader conditions of insecurity. While Campbell and Price analyse the different domains of precariousness, Vosko (2010: 2) highlights the intersecting embodiments of precarious employment, which

> is shaped by the relationship between employment status (i.e. self- or paid employment), form of employment (e.g. temporary or permanent, part-time or full-time), and dimensions of labour market insecurity, as well as social context (e.g. occupation, industry, and geography) and social location (or the interaction between social relations, such as gender, and legal and political categories, such as citizenship).

Literature is expanding on precarity in the migration field to reveal the conditions of vulnerability and insecurity that refugees and migrants confront, including their differing ability to access legal documentation (Goldring and Landolt, 2011); social rights (Gavanas and Calzada, 2016); humanitarian assistance and protection (Baban et al., 2017); and stable and legal employment. Moreover, sometimes they are compelled to inhabit certain spaces and dwellings, reconstituted as a security threat (Hodge, 2015) and targeted through forms of punishment that exhibit processes of illegalization (see also Bauder, 2014). Many studies emphasize instabilities and insecurities migrants experience in employment and workplaces, documenting migrants' 'life-worlds that are inflected with uncertainty and instability' (Waite, 2009: 416) lead to their increasing representation as the 'migrant precariat' (Schierup et al., 2014; Schierup et al., 2015).

The term 'precarious' is a relative term that is context dependent. The precarious employment migrants experience takes different forms in different societies (Tschöll, 2014: 89). For example, Goldring and Landolt's (2011) examination of migrant workers in Toronto presents a 'matrix' representing migrants' legal security and citizenship status on one axis, and their conditions and terms of employment on the other. The authors show how 'less than full citizenship status' (absence of permanent residence, restrictions on rights and entitlements, deportability and so on) can have a lasting impact on the quality of jobs that migrants obtain. Migrant status is also characterized as 'dynamic and non-linear' (Goldring and Landolt, 2011: 337), meaning that policy changes (such as the introduction of temporary migrant worker schemes) or employer strategies (such as 'flexibilization' of workforces) create movement within the matrix on both axes. The term 'context-dependent precarization' will shed light on the precarization process of Syrian refugees who probably face very little change in their precarity in Syria as seasonal labourers as in Turkey.

The uniqueness of precarity is its ability to enable the analysis of changing notions of experiences of precarization through different cultural and social domains within and across national, regional and international scales in distinct spaces of production and living conditions. I argue that the processes that generate precarity in a specific setting encapsulate both a condition of vulnerability and an element of ambiguity that simultaneously produce inclusion and exclusion. Precarity is therefore continually open to transformation and is thus unstable. Diverse actors, policies and practices produce and govern precarity, and these interventions foster further complexities and ambiguities, which in turn influence the condition of precarity.

In recent years, Syrian refugees have been employed mostly in seasonal farm work, mainly in day labouring activities, in almost all parts of rural Turkey. Their legal status, regulated under temporary protection, has granted them rights to remain in the country but has fallen short in protecting them in the labour market. Like most foreigners, Syrians also need a work permit to be employed in formal jobs (which is costly and administratively difficult, and to get a work permit, they need a job offer from an employer), and the Turkish labour market demand is for Syrian labour mostly in informal jobs. The degree of exploitation, coupled with harsh working conditions, shaped under extreme competition, leads refugees to deploy strategies to keep up with deteriorating working conditions. The most common response is to increasingly rely on female and child labour, pointing to precarization through intersecting vulnerabilities. In this regard, the role of women in the realm of social reproduction emerges as vital for a family's survival and is closely linked to the ability of Syrians to offer their labour to capitalist production.

Feminization of precarity and social reproduction

The feminization of precarity has placed more attention on the interconnectedness of production and social reproduction and on the ways capitalistic relations not only crave more women in the labour force but also absorb women's reproductive labour. It is no surprise that women mostly engage in care-related jobs. However, a gender-based transformation has taken place, where women's increasing presence in the workforce not only has challenged the notion of women as mainly devoted to domestic work for their families but also has been driving flexibilization and insecurity in the labour market. Thus, the outlook of women's work in care-related jobs is an indicator of how current capitalistic relations in the labour market – the realm of production – are based on the interaction between production and social reproduction.

This has also manifested itself in the devaluation of women's work. Feminist writers have emphasized that women's concentration in precarious jobs is not solely dependent upon a material context of jobs women engage in but also a set of cultural and ideological forces that are constantly degrading the meaning attached to the jobs done by women. Authors like Weeks (2011: 10) highlight the importance of work as a gendered matter because 'for an employee it is not merely a matter of bringing one's gendered self to work, but of becoming gendered in and through work'. Therefore, the 'precarity of feminization' needs to be pinned down to how every social activity culturally associated with the identity of women is automatically degraded and, therefore, precarized. This especially encapsulates women's reproductive labour through domestic and care work, activities that have been historically devalued, not paid and not even recognized by the current economic system as having economic value.

Focusing on women's unpaid labour, Federici (2008) criticizes the conceptualizations of precarity when they signify the homogenization of labour power by disregarding women's position and when they ignore the feminist contribution in domestic and home-based work and its role in reproducing the capitalist system. In her discussion, she refers to Hardt and Negri's concept of 'multitude' (2004).

> My concern is that the Negrian theory of precarious labor ignores, bypasses, one of the most important contributions of feminist theory and struggle, which is the redefinition of work, and the recognition of women's unpaid reproductive labor as a key source of capitalist accumulation. In redefining housework as WORK, as not a personal service but the work that produces and reproduces labor power, feminists have uncovered a new crucial ground of exploitation that Marx and Marxist theory completely ignored. All of the important political insights contained in those analyses are now brushed

aside as if they were of no relevance to an understanding of the present organization of production. (Federici, 2008)

In contemporary capitalist relations relying more and more on the productive and reproductive labour of women, migrant women have emerged on the frontline of the precarious workforce worldwide. Women now form half of the migrant population, indicating the feminization of migration. Most of them meet 'the social reproduction needs of the receiving societies' (Bakker and Gill, 2003a: 7). With the fall of Keynesian policies of social welfare, social service provisions (such as child, sick and elderly care) have been left to the market, that is, reprivatized. Economic globalization in the developing world increased cross-border mobility of women from these parts of the world in order to provide income for themselves, their families and their communities in general, a phenomenon referred to as the feminization of survival (Sassen, 2000: 504–6).

Women from developing countries thus have been migrating to the Organisation for Economic Co-operation and Development (OECD) countries and finding jobs in various sectors, such as care work and prostitution (Sassen, 2000: 506; Bakker and Gill, 2003b: 37). Migrant women are mostly employed in flexible, low-paid and informal jobs with few prospects for gaining skills or promotions. Harsh working conditions offer them few prospects for greater personal and financial autonomy, which translates into severe economic need and vulnerability at home and in the labour market. Migrant women's work in domestic and care work has gained visibility all over the world as a result of increasing job creation in the service sector. The domestic sector is regarded as potentially the largest informal sector employing migrant women. Aside from high levels of informality, another particular characteristic of this sector is the disrupted boundaries between public/private and market/non-market relations (Anderson, 2007).

Literature on migrant women and work has also focused on women's role in the reproduction of national and ethnic boundaries (Anthias and Yuval Davis, 1989; Wilford and Miller, 1998; Charles and Hintjens, 1998). Nira Yuval-Davis and Flora Anthias (1989) point out that gender divisions play a crucial role in constructing ethnic and racial divisions, an example being the central role played by women not only as biological reproducers of an ethnic group but also as its ideological reproducers, in other words, the transmitters of culture and the socializers of children (social reproducers). There is a familiar feature of women as the symbolic embodiment of ethnic/national identity and difference, constituted in no small measure by their sexual and social demeanour and their traditional role as the supporters and nurturers of men.

To elaborate more on the relationships between gender, migration and precarity, it is fruitful to refer to some earlier work by feminist scholars of migration (see Phizacklea, 1983; Morokvasic, 1984; Donato et al., 2006, among others). For example, Morokvasic (1984) stresses that in Germany although the employment rate of Turkish women was higher than that of German women, the former group was considered as not being allowed to work by their husbands. Such presumptions led to further restrictions of job offers for migrant women and also reproduced orientalist assumptions that jobs offered to migrant women would liberate them from their 'third-world' traditions (1984: 889). However, the reality was that migrant women were working in low-paid precarious work, invisible as 'dependents' and also living under the patriarchal relations of both the host society and their local community. This case depicts a combination of material and non-material forms of precarity (such as presumptions, prejudices and stereotypes about migrant women) at work.

Similarly, Freedman (2015) notes that while migrant women are generally imagined as 'vulnerable' 'victims', young men, as asylum seekers, in contrast, qualify as more 'threatening' migrants. This difference has created a trend towards 'victimization narratives' in women's asylum applications (Freedman, 2015: 17). This is another example of a non-material form of precarity, which brings about material precariousness as well. Likewise, another feminist critique of migration argues that whereas mobility through family migration is more common for women, men are more easily assumed to be abusing the system if they apply as a family member since their imagined category is a labour migrant. Some of these assumptions, prejudices and stereotypes referred to here as non-material forms of precarity may seem to benefit women at first, but they actually reproduce gender inequality and disadvantage women in the long run (Schrover and Moloney, 2013: 9 and 22).

Survival of Syrian families engaged in seasonal agricultural work is highly tied to women's work taking place in the realms of production and social reproduction. Increasing numbers of women participate in agricultural work. Regardless of Syrian women's low economic activity rate in Turkey, they participate in seasonal agricultural work in high numbers, an indicator of Syrian labour strategies to access the most precarious jobs in Turkey. Seasonal agricultural work, which has always been undertaken by the most poverty-stricken sections of society, requires women's labour in the realm not only of production but also of social reproduction. The precarization of women's labour is reflected in the increasing intensification of working hours women spend in productive and reproductive activities, as well as the degree of patriarchal control imposed on women. Both the patriarchal and capitalistic relations in local communities and the labour market take women's labour captive. While immigrant women provide cheap labour, they have no control over the wages they earn; their wages are seized as a result of the established patriarchal system in their family. This presented a radical shift from their situation of unpaid family workers and single-earner households to the agricultural proletariat.

Intersectionality and intersecting vulnerabilities

Migrant women's experience of precarity and precarization of their labour are usually depicted within the conceptual framework of intersectionality. Intersectionality has emerged within social and feminist theory as a concept to explain the 'multiple', 'complex' and/or 'intersecting' inequalities women experience in different strands of their lives. Drawing on Black women's employment experiences and on violence against women of colour, Crenshaw 'used intersectionality to describe the location of women of colour both within overlapping systems of subordination and at the margins of feminism and antiracism' (Crenshaw, 1991:1295). The concept of intersectionality is seen as an analytical tool in pointing out the logical impossibility of separating different aspects of identities and of different axes of inequality from each other.

The problem pertains to the ambiguity of the term 'intersectionality'. As Davis (2008) has observed, it is not clear whether intersectionality is a theory, a concept or a heuristic device, or a reading strategy for doing feminist analysis. 'It is not at all clear whether intersectionality should be limited to understanding individual experiences, to theorizing identity, or whether it should be taken as a property of social structures and cultural discourses' (Davis, 2008: 67). In a similar vein, Ludvig (2006: 245–58) provides insights on how to approach intersectionality and mentions a weak point in intersectionality theory. She points out that the weakness of intersectionality becomes more obvious when it is applied to empirical analysis because of the infinite nature of differences. Ludvig suggests that since the list of differences between women is endless, it is impossible to take into account all the differences that are significant at any given moment. She adds:

> Subjectively, it is often not possible for a woman to decide whether she has been discriminated against just because of her gender and or for another reason. This is precisely the problem of intersectionality: the axes of differences cannot be isolated and desegregated. (Ludvig, 2006: 245)

For that reason, she defends the idea that differences like gender, race and class do not add but multiply. In her words, 'a Black woman is not oppressed twice but many times' (Ludvig, 2006: 258).

Empirical studies exploring intersecting inequalities in different contexts are valuable in pointing to marginal voices, silenced identities by hegemonic discourses, structures and practices. Scholars like Sylvia Walby (2007), Gudrun-Axeli Knapp (2005: 254) and Joan Acker (2000) point out this necessity when they assert that analyses on intersectionality have to be connected to the structural level. The question of how race/ethnicity, class and gender are interrelated is important within a given economy and society under national, international and transnational conditions. Knapp and Acker, for example, in analysing the impact of the transfer of the triad of 'race-gender-class' from the United States into a European context, draw attention to the absence of the notion of 'class' as a category of structural inequalities in feminist theory. In the use of class, especially in the US context, more cultural notions of horizontal disparities and lifestyle differences are implied, with the assessment that the Weberian and particularly Marxist concept of class is outdated. For instance, the recent arrival of the 'race-gender-class' triad in the European context has given way to numerous studies and also policies on immigrant populations in Europe. Turkish, Arab or Algerian communities are put under scrutiny where the experiences of women from these groups, specifically their vulnerability to violent practices, are interrogated. However, a frequent approach visible in these analyses is that the experiences of immigrant women are conceived and presented not as gender inequality but as an integration problem. As Ertürk (2006) has noted, the consequences of such a conception are twofold: stigmatization and marginalization. Accordingly, immigrant women and men are further stigmatized and marginalized, which complicates their engagement in a constructive dialogue to address problems of gender inequality, which indeed exist within their communities (Ertürk, 2006).

Intersecting vulnerabilities of Syrian refugees in Turkey has been an element of their precarization. The intersectional vulnerabilities of Syrian refugees, as a form of embodiment of interconnected disadvantages based on social categorizations – such as race, ethnicity, class, gender and social status (e.g. migrants), highlight how refugees use the most vulnerable groups (such as women and children) to gain access to employment. Therefore, Syrians deploy a high number of children and women to agricultural work, not only as a strategy to obtain available jobs with more competitive wages but also as a way for the sector to have access to sources of labour that can easily be controlled and dominated.

Even though Turkey promised to combat the already-existing child wage work in agriculture, the Syrian refugee flow has exacerbated the problem of child labour and made it more difficult to implement policy solutions due to its highly informal and fragmented nature. Child workers, almost half of the agricultural workforce, are perceived to be the main workers of agriculture, and especially girls are seen to be real assets for many families. Thus, intersecting vulnerabilities are extensively visible in the exploitation of female and child labour in seasonal agricultural work in Turkey, showing the new dimension in the precarization of labour and working relations.

Work regime and bonded labour

Bonded labour in Turkey's seasonal agricultural work does not perfectly overlap with the literal definition of bonded labour, known as debt bondage. A person becomes a bonded labourer when he or she is forced to work to repay loans. Bonded labourers work long hours every day for little or no payment. They are often forced to carry out heavy tasks, for example, working in brick kilns. The actual value of work carried out by bonded labourers is often much higher than the debt owed. However, the paradox of bonded labour rests on the fact that bonded labourers rarely receive remuneration for their work (or receive very little), and they often need to borrow money to survive.[1] This form of labour is still widely practised in some parts of the world; it is estimated that there were between 18 and 20.5 million bonded labourers in 2011 (Kara, 2012). Today, bonded labourers typically work in industries that produce such goods as frozen shrimp, bricks, tea, coffee, diamonds, marble and apparel.

The different degrees of bonded labour may be explained by a distinction between 'free' and 'unfree' labour that connotes different forms of exploitation (Banaji, 2010). 'Free' labour in capitalism simply means dispossession from the means of production and subsistence. Along compatible lines, but focusing on the restructuring of class relations characterizing the neo-liberal, global era, Bernstein (2010) suggests that contemporary processes of proletarianization do not produce a proletariat as a coherent, united class but rather as different, multiple 'classes of labour'. If classes of labour have different relations to reproduction (Bernstein, 2010), reproductive realms crucially shape their very difference. In fact, a stronger focus on reproduction is necessary to understand processes of class formation. As stressed by Silvia Federici (2004, 2012) in her theorization of women's work under capitalism, the social factory always starts with reproduction. By the same token, as suggested by Maria Mies (1982, 1986), processes of dispossession and surplus extraction always start from the 'home' and the 'body' of workers. At the very least, social structures and structural differences interplay with and mediate the process of class formation (Harriss-White, 2010), as capital strategically deploys them to engage in an endless boundary-drawing process (Silver, 2003) to segment labour, cheapen its costs and subjugate it to its control. Recently, Mezzadra and Nielsen (2013) have placed further emphasis on the 'multiplication of labour' triggered by boundary-drawing strategies, conceiving borders as 'technologies of differential inclusion'. Overall, 'classes of labour' are produced by way of already 'classed' bodies as social oppression always exceeds the capitalist relation, although it powerfully structures it.

Indeed, the farm labour pool in the global agricultural workforce has come from different sources. In Turkey, it has shifted from local landless farmers in the 1950s to internally displaced Kurdish workers in the 1990s and later to migrants. As Alessandra Corrado et al. (2017) have argued, the overlapping of different sources of the labour force in the same region and its differentiation by nationality, gender and legal status has allowed labour to remain cheap and vulnerable. Together with the arrival of Syrian refugees in Turkey, 'differential inclusion' of migrant labour and labour market segmentation in Turkish agriculture is managed not only by allocating labour to different jobs but also by the competition among workers for getting existing jobs.

Seasonal agricultural work in Turkey rests upon a specific work regime in which the agricultural labour market constantly tries to include the most vulnerable labour forms and to keep that labour bonded. Practices of recruitment, retention and remuneration (3Rs) assist in bonding labour to seasonal farm work for a certain period of time. The 3Rs represent a powerful labour management regime, which Turkey's agricultural sector is currently using to fuel its integration into the world economy and to lower food production costs for the whole population. Further, the form of labour captured in the 3R work regime allows access to cheap labour without a longer-term build-up of labour institutions that would lead to better working conditions and labour solidarities. Rather, the systemic working of the 3R regime based on concentrating labour in isolated tent camps, retaining workers' wages and using labour intermediators has led to a generation of bonded workers in Turkey's seasonal agricultural labour markets.

As Peck notes, strategies of localization in terms of production processes and influence over local communities, as well as labour control, are parts of the political economy of global capitalism that are both institutionally and locally embedded (Peck, 1996). Bonded labour in Turkey's seasonal farm work is the most locally specific way to expropriate surplus. This work regime not only links productive and reproductive labour but also limits the physical movement of labour by confining workers to certain places and jobs. However, the extent of bonded labour in seasonal farm work in Turkey is a lighter version of this common 'debt bondage'. In Turkey, it is determined by the interplay of the 3Rs, which limit the mobility of labour at least for a single season of harvest.

Conclusion

The aim of this chapter has been to provide a theoretical perspective for the context-specific precarization of migrant labour. By examining three areas of precarization, intersecting vulnerabilities and work regime, it has set an understanding of how precarization of migrant labour is a dynamic process and is based on the interaction of production and social production. In this way, capitalistic relations not only push more women in the labour force but also absorb women's reproductive labour. Women and children are the two larger groups supplying precarious labour that embody the intersecting of productive and reproductive labour, and their labour is easily controlled by the patriarchal organization of their societies and capitalist system.

The concept of intersecting vulnerabilities is a path to examine how immigrant women and men are further stigmatized and marginalized, which complicates their engagement in a constructive dialogue to address problems of gender inequality, which indeed exist within their communities. As will be shown, however, the concept can help to examine the ways in which refugees use their most vulnerable groups – such as women and children – to gain access to employment in a world of work that is increasingly generating precarious job opportunities. It is also a path of examining how the working of labour markets – work regime–bonded labour – is being transformed through a bottom-up process as a result of the economic activities of migrants and their distinctive ways of social integration – vulnerable integration – into their host society.

3

Bitter lives on fertile lands

Seasonal agricultural work and migrant labour in Turkey

During the 1980s, Turkey experienced structural adjustment and change, marked by neo-liberal economic policies and major socio-economic transformations. These changes affected both urban and rural areas and populations. In the region where Turkey is located, rising transnational migration added new dimensions to these transformations and led to enduring effects on Turkey's labour markets and the agricultural sector in particular. The Turkish economy's integration into global markets and domestic social changes together affected the role of immigrant labour in Turkey's major economic sectors, such as manufacturing, services and agriculture.

Over time, in the agricultural sector, these macro transformations resulted in the gradual abolishment of family-based production and the growing need for wage workers. Seasonal workers came onto the scene to meet this need. The source of agricultural labour historically has shifted from one group to another while the constant need to reach out to the most vulnerable people has remained unchanged. In the early Republican periods, the main supply of agricultural labour came from landless farmers until the mid-1990s when they were replaced by Kurds. Internally displaced Kurds moved to urban areas but could only find work in seasonal agricultural production. Since the early 2000s, the latest group to enter into agricultural work is transnational migrants who work in the production of the most commercialized agricultural products, including hazelnuts, apricots and citrus. In these groups, Azeri and Georgian workers are absorbed into harvesting hazelnut, tea cutting and animal husbandry, mostly forming cycler migration routes between their countries and Turkey.

Immigrant workers' legal status, day-to-day work and living conditions are vivid examples of how precarity and vulnerability are woven into seasonal agricultural work for all workers. An examination of work practices of seasonal workers sheds light on the strategies the agricultural sector uses in hiring the most precarious segments of the population as a way to ensure that commercial agricultural products could be competitive in international markets. This chapter provides an overview of seasonal agricultural work and examines the significance of immigrant labour in Turkey's agricultural sector. With an aim to understand the context-specific form of precarization in seasonal agricultural labour markets, the chapter presents the main characteristics of the agricultural sector whose goal is to reach out to the most vulnerable forms of labour.

Migrant labour in the agricultural sector: A macro perspective

Globalization has radically affected how food production, distribution and consumption, as well as agricultural labour and markets, function worldwide. The liberalization of international agri-food trade and intellectual property rights on patents and seeds and the increasing importance of global retailers are the main changes that have taken place in recent decades. In the regions of Southern Europe and the Mediterranean, where Turkey is located, the structure of agriculture is characterized by increasing land fragmentation; a rising rate of permanent crops, such as olive trees, vineyards and orchards; and small farms, with low levels of technological development, from the 1970s onwards, managed by part-time or elderly farmers (Corrado et al., 2017). Over the last couple of decades, while the number of farms has steadily decreased in the region, the agricultural area and the average size of farms have grown (Papadopoulos, 2015). Coupled with this rural transformation is an increase in mechanization and expansion of irrigated areas, resulting in intensive production of fruits and vegetables. The 'artificialization' of agriculture – the intensive use of greenhouses and an excessive use of pesticides and fertilizers – has also profoundly transformed the rural landscape. Some of the MENA (Middle East and North Africa) countries – including Morocco, Tunisia and Egypt, as well as Turkey – have recently experienced similar processes of capitalization, commercialization and commoditization of land and agriculture, along with the integration of farmers in agribusiness commodity chains (Corrado et al., 2017).

Neo-liberal globalization has contributed to strengthening the power of 'food empires' (Ploeg, 2008) within vertical agri-food supply chains. The so-called retail revolution (McMichael and Friedmann, 2007) has been linked to the widespread dominance of liberalization policies. As a result of their enormous buyer power, supermarket chains not only control distribution but also decisively shape food production, processing and consumption (Burch and Lawrence, 2007). The growth of supermarket chains as 'food authorities' (Dixon, 2007) and the imposition of private standards on agricultural production through retailer-driven agri-food supply chains have had a lasting impact on agricultural production and farming systems. In their analysis of the role of supermarkets in global supply chains, Burch et al. (2013) and Richards et al. (2013) have found that in such countries as the UK, Australia and Norway, the introduction of private standards along the food chains has had the secondary effect of marginalizing small and medium family farms.

In many parts of the world, the availability of cheap and flexible migrant labour has represented a fundamental factor in restructuring the agricultural sector. A reserve of vulnerable, cheap and flexible labour has been relied on to replace family labour and to meet the pressure to lower costs and the requests of just-in-time production by agri-food chains. The 'defamilization' or individualization of farming led to the growth of wage labour, and the structural dependence on a non-local labour force has created a sharp rise in the demand for migrant labour in agriculture. In many countries, immigrant labour has met this rising demand for wage labour and filled agricultural jobs that citizens reject, 'which are often the worst paid or least secure' jobs (Bohning, 1984: 6). Labour shortages in agriculture are thus not always about the absence of labour but about the presence of workers prepared to reject the working conditions or wage levels offered (Sharma, 2006). It is no surprise that temporary migrant workers occupy these rejected jobs, given that most local workers avoid the 'three Ds': dirty, dangerous and difficult jobs (Massey, 1998).

Mezzadra and Nielsen's (2013) categories of 'multiplication of labour' and 'differential inclusion of migrants' can be observed most clearly in the agriculture sector. 'Differential inclusion' refers to the different levels of subordination, command, discrimination and segmentation defined by current border and migration regimes, which, rather than exclude, aim at 'filtering, selecting, and channelling migratory movements', through 'a huge amount of violence' (Mezzadra and Nielsen, 2013: 165). Migrant farmworkers in many countries are segmented by their legal status, nationality, gender, type of work contract and form of recruitment (Potot, 2008). The workers comprise Maghrebi, Eastern European, sub-Saharan African, South Asian and Latin American migrants. These undocumented or documented migrants, recruited through seasonal worker programmes, temporary employment agencies, informal networks or brokers, possess different types of permits and may sometimes even receive citizenship in the country of arrival. In extreme cases, they are trafficked and subject to quasi-slavery conditions.

Working under conditions deemed precarious, migrants face serious risks, having to accept low-paid jobs that pose threats to their health and safety but offer no protection or guarantees (Hess, 2006; Hartman, 2008). They also face discrimination in daily life and the labour market in their host countries. Compared to the local population, migrant workers are more often confronted with racism, ethnic discrimination, mistreatment and poor working conditions. Their experiences take a toll on their mental and physical health. In the United States, for example, which employs the most migrant agricultural labourers in the world, many migrant workers live and work with the fear of deportation, face ethnic discrimination and social exclusion and work under conditions that pose health and security threats with limited access to public services (Svensson et al., 2013).

Different countries have applied different worker recruitment models aimed at providing a cheap workforce in agriculture. Temporary work and visa programmes started to expand in the 1990s in European countries and North America, whereas some countries have regulated transnational labour mobility through private recruitment services. During the 1990s, European migratory policies became increasingly restrictive. Rural areas reflected characteristics of what has been termed the 'deportation regime' (De Genova and Peutz, 2010) of migration control. The massive presence of undocumented – 'illegalized' and thus 'deportable' (De Genova, 2002) – migrants in agriculture was one of the main reasons for the vulnerability of the entire migrant workforce. During the 2000s, the situation has slowly and partially changed. National governments have become active brokers by promoting recruitment programmes for foreign seasonal workers.[1]

Most temporary work programmes have fallen short in providing protection and security for workers but have provided an abundant supply of a cheap workforce for farmers. The major issue with visa programmes is that they constrain workers' labour mobility by limiting their work permits to a single designated employer. Migrant workers are not allowed to circulate freely in the labour market, let alone the sector in which they are employed. Transferring employers is difficult, and termination usually results in immediate deportation. Moreover, these restrictions on labour mobility grant employers tremendous power over migrants. Since most temporary visa programmes depend on a sole employer, most migrants comply with all employer requests and are reticent to raise issues regarding working and living conditions (Basok, 2003). Despite all the efforts and progress made, seasonal agricultural workers in the European Union, as elsewhere, lack decent working conditions as described by the International Labour Organization (ILO) and have to endure inadequate housing, low pay, long working hours, exploitation and discrimination.

The state of agricultural production and restructuring

Much has changed in Turkish agriculture since Turkey's founder, Kemal Atatürk, declared that 'the peasant is the lord of the nation' in the early 1930s. The 1927 Industry Census, conducted right after the foundation of the Turkish Republic, revealed that 81 per cent out of a total of thirteen million engaged in small-scale family farming[2] (Makal, 2012). Overwhelmingly family based and labour intensive, agricultural production remained intact until the introduction of mechanization through the Marshall Plan,[3] also known as the European Recovery Program, after the Second World War. Therefore, the 1950s witnessed the beginning of a structural shift from extensive to intensive agriculture, in which labour productivity increased steadily due to rising land productivity as tractors replaced traditional oxen and wooden plough. The period was also marked by a shift from subsistence crops towards cash crops and the introduction of new crops as well by the migration of the rural population to urban centres (Pamuk, 2009).

Historically, the agricultural sector has been Turkey's largest employer and a major contributor to the country's gross domestic product (GDP), exports and rural development. However, its importance has steadily been decreasing over the course of the twentieth century and into the twenty-first. Its contribution declined from 23 per cent in 1980 to 8.3 per cent in 2009 and about 5.82 per cent in 2018. Employment in agriculture has declined over the years from 50 per cent in 1980 to 19 per cent in 2018. Although agriculture has been declining in importance in relation to other service and industry sectors, it still plays a fundamental role in Turkish society, employing almost one-fifth of the population and generating income and food security for most in the country. Estimated to be the seventh-largest agricultural producer in the world, Turkey continues to be an important producer and exporter of agricultural commodities on the world market (OECD, 2011). Agricultural commodities accounted for about 10 per cent of Turkey's total exports in 2018 (FAO, 2018). The main crops are wheat, barley, corn, fruit, vegetables, nuts, tobacco, cotton and sugar. Turkey is also one of the world's largest milk producers, mainly for cheese and yogurt for domestic consumption.

With a high level of land fragmentation, nearly two-thirds of farms are smaller than 5 hectares, and the average land parcel has continued to decrease in recent decades, largely due to inheritance law and practices. Since subsistence and semi-subsistence farming is the main feature of agricultural production, it is predominantly characterized by low productivity, a high rate of hidden unemployment and a poor level of competitiveness; such farms are nonetheless crucial in providing income security and a source of livelihood for the majority of Turkey's rural population (OECD, 2011).

Over the last two decades, Turkey has undergone significant agrarian changes under the auspice of neo-liberal policies and privatization. The number of farms has steadily decreased while the rural population has shrunk and aged. Furthermore, as noted earlier, numerous farms have begun to specialize in intensive crops of fruit and vegetables with the effects of an increase in plantation density, mechanization and irrigation. The 'artificialization' of agriculture has also profoundly transformed the rural landscape (Aydın, 2010). This process has overlapped with radical changes in agricultural policy in which an aggressive overhaul took place after 2001, boosted by the elimination of price subsidies and closure of state economic enterprises, agricultural sale cooperatives and state-owned banks. These changes are mainly due to structural adjustments and trade policies under pressure from international institutions – International Monetary Fund (IMF), World Bank and World

Trade Organization (WTO) – which have favoured transnational agribusiness and financial interests (Aydın, 2010; Keyder and Yenal, 2011).

New models of agriculture where production is more closely linked to global markets (Nieto, 2014) and where there is greater dependence on wage labour and internal migration have been emerging in many parts of rural Turkey. The intensive marketization of Turkish agricultural production has left small farmers vulnerable to the risks of market fluctuations and global price competition. The result has been the overexploitation of farmers' labour, non-agricultural income diversification and greater use of wage labour rather than unpaid family labour, coupled with quality production and multifunctionality and differentiation of products. The following sections evaluate seasonal agricultural work, as a form of dominant working practice, to fully understand the dynamics of the precarization of seasonal farm work in Turkey.

Seasonal agricultural work: Patterns, numbers and regulations

Farm work was traditionally designated to a particular region of south-eastern Turkey where large landholding is common and landless farmers' labour was necessary. For the rest of the country, unpaid family workers were the essential labour source; when extra labour was needed, farming families relied on traditional collective labour practices, such as *imece*[4] and *icar*.[5] The first seasonal farmworkers were brought from Sudan by Kavalali Ibrahim Pasha[6] in the 1890s to be employed on the Çukurova Plantation where cotton farms started intensive production for world markets in the province of Adana (Çınar, 2012). Until the 1990s, seasonal agricultural workers were not a significant and noticeable presence in Turkey. Both the disappearance of conventional production relations and the increase in cultivated areas of high-value crops, which mostly need manual labour for hoeing and harvesting, inevitably boosted the demand for seasonal migrant workers.

Farm wage work takes different forms, but the most widespread is seasonal. Seasonal agricultural work is undertaken by local or migrating workers. While local workers undertake agricultural work where they reside or in close vicinity, seasonal migratory workers move from their usual place of residence to other provinces to work. Especially during peak production periods, seasonal workers travel with their families from one area to another and their migration pattern can be a cycle of six to nine months per year (Support to Life, 2014; GNAT, 2015). The mobility pattern of a seasonal worker family is based on an annual cycle of moving from, for example, a sugar beet harvest in central Anatolia in April, to a vegetable and cherry harvest in May and June in Afyon, to hazelnuts and apricots in July and August in Ordu, Giresun, Rize, to citrus in Adana in October and November. Figure 3.1 shows the map of Turkey's provinces where main cash crops are produced and hence the demand for seasonal workers.

The demand for seasonal workers is high in many regions of Turkey. The main regions and products that have already been researched are hazelnuts in the Black Sea region; fresh vegetables in the Aegean; citrus fruits, fresh vegetables and cotton in the Çukurova region; and onions, legumes, sugar beets and apricots in central Anatolia. Workers perform such tasks as hoeing, picking and drying crops and spreading them out in the sun. Starting in March or April, migrating worker families gather together to form a large group of family members, including women, children and the elderly, to travel from one region to the next to work on harvesting different crops produced in different regions (MIGA, 2012).

To date, the exact number of seasonal workers is unknown, but Household Labour Force Data of TURKSTAT estimates that in 2014, 5.4 million workers in Turkey were engaged in agricultural production, 485,000 of whom were engaged in agricultural production seasonally for wages. Their number has estimated to reach to 1–1.5 million as seasonal workers travel to work (GNAT, 2015; MIGA, 2012; Support to Life [Hayata Destek], 2014). Note that this estimation does not include Syrians, Azerbaijanis, Afghans and Georgians working in Turkish agriculture – only those seasonal workers.

Seasonal agricultural work is informal work done by the most deprived groups who remain largely outside of legal regulations and protection. Most significantly, agricultural workers remain outside of the protection of Turkish Labour Law No 4857, because the workers who are employed in agricultural and forestry enterprises with fewer than fifty workers and job durations shorter than thirty days are beyond its scope. Lack of protection and security are some of the foremost indicators of seasonal agricultural work. However, in recent years small but important steps have been taken through raised awareness resulting from traffic and workplace accidents and the work of international organizations to make employers in the agricultural supply chain comply with human and worker rights.

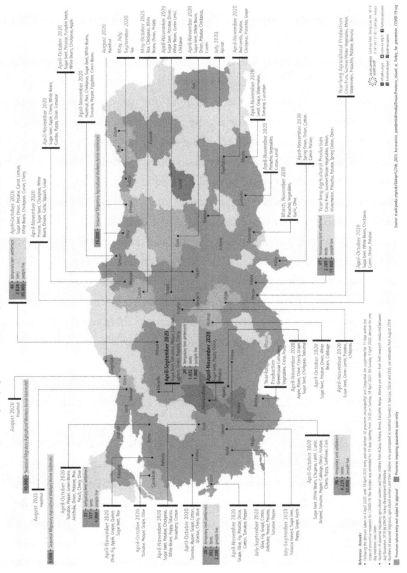

Figure 3.1 Turkey's map of cash crops and demand for seasonal agricultural workers. Source: Development Workshop Archive.

The most important piece of regulation, the Prime Ministerial Circular for the Improvement of Working and Living Conditions of Seasonal Migratory Agricultural (METİP), published in 2010, was designed to organize seasonal farm work and compensate for the exclusions with Labour Law 4857. The circular makes some arrangements for the improvement of current living, transportation, shelter, health care, education and security conditions of seasonal migratory workers. The METİP project also assigns special duties and roles to central and local governments to provide better living and working conditions. However, these regulations have not been effective in battling against informality; for example, they have had no influence on increasing labour inspections and ensuring a minimum wage. While METİP has made the security problem of seasonal workers visible, it has also ended up relegating these workers into special tent areas that are mostly designed to reduce interaction between local populations and migrant workers to a minimum, thereby preventing ethnic-based conflict (KEIG, 2015). METİP is seen as a tool of the Turkish state to control and register Kurdish workers travelling from the south-eastern part of the country. METİP falls short in protecting all seasonal workers and has had a regional focus mostly in the Black Sea provinces where hazelnut production takes place and a response to the multinational cooperations' concerns in keeping their supply chains clean of child labour and other poor labour standards.

Seasonal agricultural workers: Bitter lives on fertile lands

In his well-acclaimed novel *On Fertile Lands* (1953), Turkish author Orhan Kemal describes the bitter and merciless living and working conditions that day labourers in the Çukurova region[7] endured just to earn a piece of bread in the 1940s and 1950s. The majority of Kemal's day labourers were from landless farming families. Winners and losers on fertile lands have not changed much since the days that Kemal's novel portrays; only the type of workers have undergone transition with local landless farming families being replaced by seasonal agricultural workers travelling from south-eastern Turkey to the Çukurova region. Kurdish and Arab workers from the provinces of Şanlıurfa, Adıyaman and Mardin have been prominent in seasonal agricultural work since the beginning of the 1990s. However, since early 2011, these workers from south-eastern Turkey have been replaced by a new labour source: Syrian refugees.

Increasingly relying on wage labour has been the response of both smallholders and landless rural families to changing household needs and composition. The presence of farm wage workers in Turkey did not become a significant and noticeable phenomenon until the mid-1990s, when internal conflict broke out between Turkish security forces and the Kurdistan Workers Party (PKK), resulting in massive displacement of the Kurdish population from south-eastern Anatolian villages. Many Kurdish villages were evacuated, leading to an immense wave of migration from eastern and south-eastern provinces to western Turkey. Most of the displaced population migrated to metropolitan peripheries, notably Istanbul, Ankara, Izmir, Bursa, Mersin and Adana. Those who lacked kinship networks in these urban centres settled in south-eastern cities, such as Batman, Diyarbakır, Şanlıurfa, Şırnak and Mardin (Yıldırım, 2014: 202). Due to high unemployment rates in these cities, they quickly became seasonal migrant workers (Keyder and Yenal, 2013: 145). They work seasonally in northern, southern and western regions of Turkey for six to eight months every year and spend the winter unemployed in their hometowns (Özbek, 2007: 34–8; Pelek, 2010: 61–3). Both neo-liberal agrarian policies and forced migration turned Kurdish farmers into the most important agrarian labour source since the 1990s. Many studies indicate that Kurdish workers earned the lowest wages and had the worst living and working conditions (Özbek, 2007; Çınar, 2012; Yıldırım, 2014).

In the 2000s, seasonal work has turned to more diverse worker groups from different ethnic groups within Turkey and immigrants. Four main worker groups are identified, including internal migrants, local farmers, immigrants and refugees (Dedeoğlu, 2018). First, Turkish Kurds, Turkish Arabs and Turkish Romans have comprised an internal migrant worker group who travel across regions and cities and return home when the job is over (Mura, 2016: 118). Second, non-migrant workers – generally called local workers, whose ethnic origin is mostly Turkish – are employed in places close to their homes. They are mostly small landowners who do extra work after they complete their own harvest (Pelek, 2019). The third group comprises immigrants from Georgia and Azerbaijan, who started to migrate to Turkey after the Soviet Union's dissolution. They come to Turkey with tourist visas and work temporarily in agrarian jobs without working permits (see Section 3.5

Figure 3.2 Seasonal agricultural tent settlement in Adana. Source: Development Workshop Archive.

and Dedeoğlu, 2018). The final group is Syrian refugees, the subject of this book (Figure 3.2).

The most distinct characteristic of seasonal agricultural work is the type of households that undertake it. The 2014 Support to Life Association study, which surveyed 1,353 individuals (49.7 per cent women, 50.3 per cent men), shows that the average seasonal agricultural household size is seven. Of the 168 households surveyed, 50 per cent consist of seven or fewer members, while a quarter consists of ten or more members. These household sizes indicate that the number of children per mother is high or that close relatives come together to form a single familial unit for the purpose of composing a team for seasonal agricultural work. Another distinctive character of worker families is the young age composition. While 35 per cent of the total population studied are between the ages of nineteen and forty-five, only 11 per cent are over the age of forty-six. In total, the proportion of those aged under twenty-five years to the total is 68 per cent. The young age is reflected in the average age, which is twenty-two (Support to Life, 2014).

Women and children are an important component of the seasonal labour force. Turkish agricultural production has been highly feminized since the early days of urban migration, starting in the late 1950s. Years later, seasonal agricultural work is still highly characterized by feminization. As described by Çınar (2014), women are the most desirable workforce for seasonal work as women, and their labour are governed more easily by traditional patriarchal roles and depend on the hierarchical chain of paternal relations. This results in increased control over women's labour and bodies and confiscation of the fruits of their labour. Women generally take part in agricultural work not as individuals but as an extension of their family or household (Çınar, 2014: 181).

Two of the most debated topics in the literature on seasonal agricultural work are women workers and child labour. Studies unveil the length of workdays women endure: in addition to work in the fields, most of the cooking, cleaning and taking care of children fall on women's shoulders (Çınar, 2014; Çelik et al., 2015). Women work for sixteen to eighteen hours per day on average, their most vital helpers being their daughters. These girls undertake most of the in-house chores: cooking, baking bread, carrying water, collecting firewood, building fires, cleaning the tent and so on. In addition, some take over the care responsibilities of their younger siblings (KEİG, 2015). In general, since agricultural work is generally informal work, female workers work without any social security coverage, let alone maternal insurance. Unsanitary conditions, low socio-economic status, marrying young and adolescent and frequent pregnancies that usually follow, lack of access to health care during and after pregnancy due to remote housing, all contribute to increased risks to maternal and infant health that can lead to illness or even death.

Labour intermediaries are important actors in regulating seasonal agricultural labour markets in Turkey. A labour intermediary (*dayıbaşı* or *elci* locally) is usually a former agricultural worker with strong local connections and social capital. A middleman can have worker teams composed of 30–150 people, dependent on his power to recruit and his ability to sustain work arrangements. Generally, his responsibilities consist of ensuring that workers arrive on time and work properly each labour day, accommodating workers by helping them to set up their tents or by arranging a tentative place and solving any disagreement between workers and employers. After the job is accomplished, the employer pays the total sum of wages to the labour intermediary. Then, the latter distributes the money to workers after cutting his share, including his extra expenses, such as loans or travel payments lent to the workers. He receives a commission of around 10 per cent from each worker's daily wage; in other words,

Figure 3.3 A group of seasonal agricultural workers at work. Source: Development Workshop Archive.

labour intermediaries earn no salary from the employer (the Support to Life, 2014: 63). The rest of their practices, including the labour process, types of remuneration, duration of work in each field or in each region and conditions of travel and accommodation, differ immensely according to the product, region and field (Figure 3.3).

Competition among the poor: Migrant workers in the agricultural sector

Prior to the arrival of Syrians in 2011, the most visible immigrant workers in Turkey were Azerbaijanis in Kars and Ardahan, where livestock rearing is widespread and Georgians actively participate in harvesting hazelnuts and tea in the Black Sea region. After their arrival, Syrians began to work in many diverse agricultural sectors in several provinces: for example, Antalya, Mersin and Adana, known as 'citrus provinces', where Syrians dominate agricultural work; and the cotton-producing provinces of Adana, Şanlıurfa and Hatay, as well as in the Aegean region, where vegetables and fruits especially are produced. In this section, I will only focus on Georgian and Azerbaijani workers to better illuminate existing competition between worker groups in seasonal work before I turn to Syrian agricultural workers in the rest of the book.

My fieldwork revealed three main migrant groups dispersed into three main geographical regions. First, Georgian workers harvest hazelnuts and tea in the Black Sea region, where an easy passage through the Sarp border is provided with a liberal visa policy signed between the two countries. The second migrant group is Azeris, who are the main labour supplier for animal and livestock husbandry in the cities of Kars and Ardahan of the northeast region. The last migrant group, Syrians, is predominantly found in south-eastern cities of Turkey, where intensive and large-scale farming and production takes place throughout the year. Geographical dispersion of certain migrant groups is determined by their proximity to their home countries and border gates from where migrants travel to Turkey. It is also influenced by migrant networks and social ties established with local communities.

Georgian workers: Harvesting hazelnuts and tea

Human movement between Turkey and Georgia has been growing since the early years of Georgia's independence in 1991 and has taken a radical turn after the two countries signed the visa waiver agreement in 2006. The agreement allows people from both countries to travel across the border for 90 days within a total of 180 days with only a valid national ID; a passport is not needed. In 2017, with this liberal visa policy in place, Turkey introduced a ninety-day work permit for Georgian agricultural workers. Over 2 million Georgians visit Turkey every year, with 2.4 million crossing the border in 2017. This is quite a significant flow since the total population of Georgia was only 4.9 million that year. The Sarp border gate is the most frequently used crossing point between Turkey and Georgia. Workers use that gate to enter Turkey for the hazelnut and tea harvesting seasons. A total of 94.3 per cent of all border crossings from Georgia into Turkey occur at the Sarp gate, and its distribution by months shows that May, July, August and September are the peak months during which hazelnuts and tea are harvested in the Black Sea region.

Georgia's economic and political instability has led to frequent cyclical migration to be a 'national strategy' for Georgian households, with Turkey as a popular destination. Short-term, cyclical or seasonal labour migration has become the main characteristic of Georgian migration to Turkey (Badurashvili, 2012).

Georgian migrants depend on Georgian-ethnic origin citizens of Turkey for networking and making initial contact. While Georgians are the single ethnic group in tea harvesting, they pick hazelnuts alongside workers from southeastern Turkey. Georgians form a type of circular migration in which their tourist visas[8] obtained at the border allow them to stay for a three-month period during which they work in tea and hazelnut harvesting (ÇAYSİAD, 2015; Ulukan and Ulukan, 2011).

Georgian women are the favourable workers of the hazelnut harvest while men typically engage in the tea harvest and construction work. In most cases, migrants work for the same farmers every year in a village and are housed in village houses or in huts provided by farmers. Recruitment of workers is usually conducted through agricultural labour intermediaries and social networks of migrants. Well-known Georgian labour intermediaries find workers for farmers and jobs for migrants. During my fieldwork, I interviewed a Georgian labour intermediary who had a pool of workers ready for work. I met him at a coffeehouse where he also made his business connections with farmers who were ready to harvest their hazelnut trees; he agreed with a couple of them to send a group of workers the next day to harvest hazelnuts. Georgians are one of the major international groups working in Turkey's agriculture with a privileged status to have work permit exemption, if registered, and visit Turkey every year to work in hazelnut and tea harvest.

Azerbaijani workers: 'One nation, two states'

Turkey has also been a popular destination for Azerbaijanis since the 1990s. It is common to meet and see Azeris in Turkish daily life and on popular TV shows. Their high social visibility is mostly the result of the national origin and language Turks and Azeris share, leading to great social acceptance and toleration of Azeris. Shared ethnic, historical, cultural and social ties have led to a high volume of Azeri migration to Turkey following Azerbaijan's independence in 1992. Azeris and Turks share a Turkish-language base, therefore easier communication. The visa agreement between Turkey and Azerbaijan has facilitated easy entry and exit from both sides. Azeris can visit Turkey without needing a visa for a thirty-day period. Besides easy air travel, direct coach services run regularly between Turkey and Azerbaijan, especially from Nahcivan, Baku and Ganja. Lax bureaucratic inceptions and authorities turning a blind eye to undocumented and irregular[9] immigrants have allowed Azeris to take up informal jobs in Turkey.

The number of those entering Turkey from Azerbaijan increased rapidly in the early 2000s, surpassing 650,000 in 2014, and dropping slightly to 600,000 in 2016. About one-third of those who enter (around 200,000 in 2016) come through the Dilucu border gate between the autonomous region of Nakhchivan and Turkey. A detailed record of monthly entrances from the Dilucu border gate in 2016 shows that July, August and September have recorded the highest entrance numbers, months during which the provinces of Kars and Ardahan demand the most labour. A middle-aged (forty-five) Azeri man, acting as a labour intermediary for Azeris to come to Turkey and find jobs in agriculture, tells the story of labour migration from Nakhchivan:

> Nakhchivan has [a population of] 375,000. I have come and gone for twenty years. Kars, Iğdır, Antalya, Istanbul – I have been to all of these places. My village has fifty souls, here there are hundreds of souls. There are three or four people here from every village. I have worked in every job: agriculture, construction. However, the month-long visa is very short. You come here, work for a few days, then it rains and you cannot get work. The month-long visa is not enough. It is too short. These are kind people; they do not wish ill of anyone. Turkey is the number one [country] in the world. Had it not been for Turkey, we would not have existed!

The demand for Azeri labour is high in the provinces of Kars and Ardahan, where raising livestock and animal husbandry are the main agricultural enterprises. The region's soaring popularity for cheese products and intensive urban migration necessitates the use of migrant labour in many production activities. The presence of ethnic Azeris in Turkey, Azeri's ability to communicate in Turkish and the geographical proximity of Nakhchivan facilitate a cyclical migration for Azeri workers who arrive in the region in early April and work until snowfall in October, working in such activities as animal husbandry and grass cutting. Usually arriving as men's crews, migrants work for the same employer every year; migrants and employers rely on close and trusting relationships. The relationship built over the year is an important asset for both parties. As one farmer says: 'If a guy's visa was up last year, he took a break from work to go back to his country and to renew his visa. He left his money here and collected it when he returned.' The close ties between the two countries have had a lasting impact on migratory flow from Azerbaijan to

Turkey but had little impact on improving working and living conditions of Azeri workers in Turkish agricultural production.

Conclusion

In many countries, agricultural jobs are filled with immigrant labour who are willing to accept often the worst paid or least secure jobs. Recruitment of migrant workers is organized by many different strategies ranging from seasonal worker programmes, temporary employment agencies, informal networks or brokers. In extreme cases, they are trafficked and subject to quasi-slavery conditions. Due to precarious working conditions in agricultural production, migrants face serious risks and most of the time feel compelled to accept these low-paid jobs that pose threats to their health and safety but offer no protection or guarantees.

In Turkey, the emergence of seasonal agricultural workers in the mid-1990s after the demise of family-based agricultural production is one of the major changes that took place. The source of agricultural labour is extensively diversified as many worker groups coming from different backgrounds have been competing for agricultural jobs. Kurdish and Arab groups from Urfa, Mardin and Diyarbakır, followed by immigrants from Syria, Georgia and Azerbaijan, are the major worker groups in Turkey. Migrant labour is usually sourced from Syria, Azerbaijan and Georgia and clustered around specific geographic regions of Turkey. While migrant labour from Syria, Azerbaijan and Georgia has been important for the precarization of the seasonal agricultural workforce, this trend is enforced through the cultivation of antagonistic relations between different segments of agricultural wage workers and competition for jobs among the poor.

While it is clear that migrant labour has been playing an important role in agricultural production since the early 2000s in Turkey, their working and living conditions are a vivid case of how precarity and vulnerability are woven into seasonal agricultural work for all workers. Not only migrants but also Turkish workers endure these conditions through which the agricultural sector reproduces the cycle of poverty among agricultural workers. Seasonal agricultural work requires a highly mobile labour force moving from the places where they usually reside to sites where agricultural production takes place; it is also based on teamwork, with teams composed of ten to fifteen people working together. Therefore, migrant workers generally move together with all members of their families and relatives so that they can form a team of workers to take up jobs. Most of these practices organizing seasonal work in Turkey are also relevant for migrants and integrate migrant labour into the production process.

4

Syrians in Turkey

From guests to refugees

When the Syrian war broke out in 2011, former prime minister Recep Tayyip Erdoğan declared: 'Insallah, we will shortly go to Damascus, we will read Fatiha at the tomb of Saladin-i Eyyubi and we will do our prayers in the Umayyad Mosque' (Hürriyet, 2012). His declaration revealed the expectation for a quick victory. However, before the good news of triumph in Syria, a massive flock of Syrians arrived at the Turkish border seeking safe refuge. In the early days of the Syrian crisis, the Turkish government welcomed Syrians as guests and responded to the emergency situation by placing them in newly constructed refugee camps, providing key protection and humanitarian assistance.

This chapter offers an overview of the current state of Syrian refugees in Turkey and an analysis of structural factors influencing the precarization of Syrians in the Turkish labour market. The majority of Syrians live outside of refugee camps in host communities where they face harsh, insecure and precarious conditions. They are entangled in a multifaceted and shifting set of relations – legal, governmental and humanitarian – and encounter multiple pathways to precarity, differential inclusion and negotiated citizenship status. Syrians' situation has widely and for a long time been treated as a humanitarian problem, but it has so far turned into a long-term integration problem that demands effective policy responses. Syrians' labour market participation is the strongest indicator of how they are integrated into Turkish society. Existing conditions of legal rights available to Syrians have built up two different pathways to integration: formal and informal. Through formal integration refugees are able to make claims to citizenship rights, as well as negotiate access to employment, humanitarian assistance and social services. Through precarious, informal integration Syrians are becoming an indispensable part of labour-intensive industries through which Turkey enters global competition in a constant search of tapping into cheap forms of labour.

Syrians in Turkey: A demographic overview

As the war intensified in Syria, Turkey hosted more and more Syrians, with their numbers exceeding three million over the years. As of summer 2020, 3.5 million Syrians were registered in Turkey under temporary protection, but the figure was estimated to be approximately five million when unregistered, irregular and undocumented Syrians were also counted. Syrians in Turkey are heterogeneous in terms of ethnicity, religion, gender, generation, social class and so on. There are Kurdish, Turkmen, Arab, Shi'ite, Dom, Bedouin, Armenian, Yazidi, Assyrian and Syrian nationals; Palestinian and Iranian refugees coming from Syria; working-, middle- and upper-class Syrians; and Syrians from diverse religious backgrounds, including Christian and Muslim Alawites and Sunnis, and Shi'ite settled in various cities of Turkey (Şimşek, 2018).

When Syrians first arrived in large numbers, they initially settled in border cities, such as Urfa, Hatay, Kilis and Gaziantep. However, after almost eight years, Istanbul now hosts the largest number of Syrians, followed by Gaziantep, Hatay and Urfa. As of May 2020, Istanbul has 496,775 Syrians, along with migrants from Somalia, Russia, Afghanistan, Iraq, Iran, Bangladesh, Uzbekistan and Moldova, among others. The cities of Kilis, Hayat, Gaziantep and Urfa host the largest number of refugees (around 50 per cent) as a proportion of their total population. The dispersion of Syrians to Adana, Mersin, Izmir and Bursa is mostly the result of available employment opportunities in these cities and of the relocation of many from border cities to megacities. Only 63,403 refugees live in government-run camps, while the majority live in host communities in self-reliant households (DGMM, 2020).

The demographic characteristics of Syrians in Turkey are significant in assessing their migration patterns and labour market activities. Contrary to the trends appearing in the male-dominated refugee movement to Europe, women make up 46 per cent of the total Syrian population living in Turkey (DGMM, 2020), indicating a family-based migratory pattern. Supporting this family pattern, children make up a large percentage of Syrians in Turkey, with 47 per cent under the age of eighteen and 30 per cent under the age of ten of the total Syrian population. Although refugee men are more visible in public, the data strongly indicate that women and youth comprise a large portion of the Syrian population in Turkey. Hostility towards the Syrian population in Turkey is usually reasoned with the argument of why Syrian men had fled Syria instead of joining the war to defend their country. This not only sheds light on the visibility of Syrian men but also hides the invisible groups, such as women and children, in the Syrian population in Turkey.

Syrians' educational and occupational qualifications are another public policy concern, in particular whether only those with low education and qualifications stay in Turkey but those with higher qualifications move to other European countries. The Syrian Barometer, which is the largest survey on Syrians, conducted with 7,591 people in Turkey above the age of 18 in 2017 shows that 18.5 per cent were illiterate, 11.8 per cent were literate but with no formal education and 28 per cent were primary school graduates. Almost 60 per cent of the sample had low educational qualifications, whereas only 7 per cent of those surveyed were university graduates (Erdoğan, 2018). Research results on income levels of Syrian families when back in Syria show that 60 per cent declared themselves in the middle-income range and 17 per cent with above-middle income and only 13 per cent with lower-income level (Erdoğan, 2018).

A cursory look at Syrians' main demographic characteristics reveals significant information about age distribution, gender composition and educational features that all bear implications for their labour market activities and decisions on who can work and what types of jobs they can engage in. The data indicate that children aged between fourteen and eighteen years and possibly women are the prime candidates to work in clandestine, informal jobs offering low wages, harsh working conditions and long hours with few security measures. Not only educational qualifications but also their legal status affect their access to employment, as deskilling among educated and qualified migrant workers is no surprise.

Temporary protection: Legal framework and migration policies

Until 2014, Turkey lacked the apparatus to legally protect Syrians as Turkey is one of the few states in the world to sustain the geographic limitation clause of the 1951 Refugee Convention, which stipulates that refugee status will only be granted to individuals coming from European countries. This geographical limitation relegates applications from non-European countries to 'asylum seeker' while thousands of non-Europeans reside in Turkey with the hope of receiving formal or refugee status from other countries (Erdoğan, 2015). Also, the Settlement Law of Turkey (1934 İskan Kanunu), which draws the main frame of Turkey's migration policies, is based on a nation-building notion in which only those of Turkish descent are accepted as migrants coming to settle and others are viewed as 'foreigners' or, as in the case of irregular migrants, as 'tourists'. The result is that in the early stages of Syrian influx in 2011, the Turkish government accepted Syrians as guests with the expectation that they would return to Syria soon once the conflict was over.

Turkey's peculiar migration policies presented many obstacles for Syrians in claiming refugee status and permanent residence. Yet, after recognizing the unique challenges posed by such a large influx of people in such a short period of time, the Turkish government introduced a series of measures aimed at providing legal status to Syrians in order to address their long- and short-term needs. One year after the enactment of the Law on Foreigners and International Protection (No. 6458) in 2013, the Turkish government issued the Regulation on Temporary Protection, which applies specifically to Syrian refugees and others who arrive en masse and whose application for protection cannot be processed individually. This regulation granted Syrians residency, identification cards and access to basic social services, such as education and health care.

A *kimlik* (ID card) is needed to activate the rights associated with temporary protection (TP) and to access certain social services. A *kimlik* is required to register with a local office of the Directorate General for Migration Management (DGMM). But holding a *kimlik* does not result in permanent residency nor in the right to apply for citizenship. TP does not provide 'residency permits' or any stipulation for length of stay in Turkey that may lead to achieving permanent status (Kutlu, 2015). Since the *kimlik* is location specific, if a Syrian moves to another city, they need to inform the Turkish authorities of the move in advance in order to cancel their *kimlik* in one location and re-register for another in the new location.

Upon receiving a *kimlik*, Syrian refugees are able to access certain limited social rights – for example, access to free health care and education for children – often similar to those provided to Turkish citizens. Basic healthcare services are covered, including doctor visits, necessary surgery and 80 per cent of all drug costs (Kutlu, 2015). The *kimlik*, however, does not provide any assistance towards accommodation costs, which contribute to everyday forms of precarity. For example, outside of the camps, families must cover the high costs of housing, especially high in urban centres such as Istanbul. Most Syrians live in overcrowded houses, flats and makeshift arrangements, such as tents, decayed buildings, wedding halls, barns or abandoned prison sites. Agricultural work paves the way for Syrians to avoid high accommodation costs and these makeshift arrangements by providing tent settlements in rural Turkey. In recent years, the Syrians with a *kimlik* are also given *a Kızılay card*, the Emergency Social Safety Net (ESSN), which is recharged monthly and can be used at shops to buy food and other essentials, or at ATMs to withdraw cash. The amount of money on each card is based on family size, with each family member adding a value of 120 Turkish lira (TRY) (about 17 Euros) to the monthly allowance (Cupolo, 2017).

The Law on Work Permits for Foreigners under TP was issued on 15 January 2016. It allows refugees to apply to the Ministry of Family, Labour and Social Services for work permits six months after they register for TP status. Since 2016, the number of work permits issued to Syrians[1] has been limited to a few people: for example, in 2018, out of a total of 115,837 work permits issued, only 34,573 were given to Syrians (MoFWSS, 2020). Work permits represent only a small portion of Syrians living in Turkey. According to the TP legislation, refugees cannot be paid less than the minimum wage, and the ratio of refugee workers cannot exceed 10 per cent of the total number of Turkish employees in a given workplace. However, those who work in agriculture and husbandry as seasonal workers are exempt from work permit requirements. Exempting agriculture paves the way for Syrians to be employed freely, even on informal terms, thereby making it difficult to estimate the rise in the number of Syrian agricultural workers.

While significantly improving Syrians' status from mere guests and building up Syrians' formal integration channels into Turkish society through access to basic services and rights, these regulations have nevertheless fallen short in protecting them fully. Limited access to formal employment opportunities and costly and administratively difficult-to-obtain work permits have undermined the formal protection offered to Syrians through the TP legislation and opened up ways for their concentration in the informal labour force in Turkey, including agricultural work. Their limited opportunities and protections have contributed to everyday forms of precarity and precarization in the labour market.

Labour market integration of refugees and Syrian labour

For refugees, the right to work is key to becoming self-reliant, thus enabling them to build their lives in their new homes and secure dignity and allowing them to contribute to their host communities. Refugees' labour market integration is now more important than ever since forced migration has reached the highest ever level, with 79.5 million people seeking protection in the European Union and other parts of the world in 2019, a number that is expected to continue to grow. The annual Global Trends report of the United Nations High Commissioner for Refugees (UNHCR) shows that out of this huge population of forcible displacement as a result of persecution, conflict or generalized violence, 25.4 million are refugees, 40 million are internally displaced people and 3.1 million are asylum seekers. Under UNHCR's mandate, developing regions hosted 85 per cent of the world's refugees of around 16.9 million people. Since early 2011, Turkey hosted the largest number of refugees worldwide, with 3.5 million people (UNHCR, 2020). Against this increasing refugee flow, of the 145 states that have been part of the 1951 Refugee Convention, almost half have declared reservations; even states that grant the right to work usually impose conditions on access to labour markets. The same limitations apply to many of the forty-eight states that are not ratified with the Refugee Convention (Zetter et al., 2017). These constraints force refugees to use irregular paths both to enter and to work in their host country. Even in countries that adhere to the convention, the legal entitlement to work for refugees is rarely unconditional.

While mostly relegated to informal labour market activities, migrants typically do not take jobs away from domestic workers (Constant, 2014), do not depress the wages of the natives (Peri, 2014) and do not abuse the welfare system (Giulietti, 2014). A study by Peschner and Tanay (2017) illustrates that the overall performance of refugees/asylum seekers is better than those of migrants who came with family reunification status but falls significantly behind those who migrated through work status. Thus, refugees have lower employment rates than most other migrant groups: lower than natives (56 per cent vs 65 per cent as an EU average) and much lower than those who have come for employment and study (71 per cent) (Peschner and Tanay, 2017). Women asylum seekers have a relatively low rate of participation in the labour market. They cannot access opportunities for cultural integration, language and skills training and employment due to the burden of child care and foreign cultural codes (European Parliament, 2016).

Lower labour market integration is usually associated with institutional barriers placed before refugees, and refugees' legal status upon entry into the host country has a long-lasting effect on their labour market potential (Constant and Zimmermann, 2005). Once their status is approved and they gain the right to settle, asylum seekers receive higher pay and work for longer hours than other migrant groups. This is thought to be a result of asylum seekers being more likely to invest in human capital once they have been granted asylum and settle permanently. The case of Syrian refugee agricultural workers in Turkey, however, shows that the structure and conditions in the labour market can lead to further precariousness for refugee labour and an informal path of labour market integration even when refugees have the legal right to settle.

Permanent precarization of Syrian labour in Turkey

Syrians' labour market activities have received growing interest from scholars of diverse backgrounds who try to understand the implications of this unprecedented population mobility for the Turkish labour market. A recent ILO Ankara report finds that out of 2 million Syrians of working age in Turkey, 813,000 were employed (including 130,000 self-employed). This represents 2.8 per cent of the employed population in Turkey. The employment rate of Syrians is approximately 40 per cent. More than 97 per cent of Syrian workers work informally. Formally employed women are a very small share of the workforce (ILO Ankara Office, 2020). Syrian workers are concentrated in a few provinces (Istanbul, Adana, Bursa, Gaziantep, Hatay, Konya and Izmir). Working Syrians in these provinces account for 84 per cent of all working Syrians in Turkey. Syrians are more likely than informally employed Turkish workers to work in companies with ten or more employees. While more than 75 per cent of

Syrians work more than forty-five hours per week (legal weekly working time in Turkey), they earn less than the minimum wage on average.[2]

It is no surprise that labour-intensive informal sectors – agriculture, textiles, clothing, livestock, construction and tourism – popularly employ Syrian workers in a constant search for new forms of labour to lower production costs (Dedeoğlu, 2012 and 2014; Dedeoğlu and Gökmen, 2011; Kaymaz and Kadkoy, 2016; Afanasieva, 2016). Most qualitative studies have pointed to the strong presence of Syrian labour in informal and marginal jobs, while quantitative research has questioned if Syrians have had any impact on native-born Turkish workers and wage levels. Ceritoğlu et al. (2017) find that the prevalence of informal employment in Turkey, which stands around 35 per cent, has accelerated the diffusion of the immigrant workforce into informal jobs. Del Carpio and Wagner (2015) support this finding by showing that the presence of Syrian refugees has led to large-scale displacement of Turkish workers from the informal sector, around six natives for every ten refugees. Displacement occurs among all types of informally employed Turkish workers irrespective of their gender, age and level of education. Together with the increasing employment of Syrians in informal sector jobs, Turkish citizens with no formal education have especially experienced significant job losses in the informal sectors.

The frankest statement on Syrian migrant employment in Turkey comes from the current mayor of Gaziantep and former minister of Family and Social Policies, Fatma Şahin, during an interview in 2014: 'The 140,000 Syrians in Gaziantep have been like a tonic for the factories' (Erdoğan, 2015: 80). This is the acknowledgement of downward effect on wage level of Syrians integration into informal jobs, which is observed in many labour-intensive sectors as well as in agriculture. In large cities, such as Gaziantep, Adana, Bursa and İstanbul, Syrians work mostly in textiles and apparel workshops. In recent years, Syrians have been especially attracted to Istanbul due to work opportunities in clothing sweatshops.

Working conditions fall far short of decent, demonstrating that Turkey is not a place of escape for Syrians but a new place of struggle. Syrians work for lower wages than local workers. Interviews conducted by Ercüment Akdeniz in İstanbul show that Syrians earn TRY 70–100 less per week than local workers (Akdeniz, 2014: 35). Employment of Syrian migrants, especially children, in informal 'under-the-counter' workshops frequently attracts attention not only in Turkey but also in the international press, due to the global supply chain of the international trade markets that are produced in these workshops. According to a Reuters story, Syrian children contribute to the upkeep of their families by working in textiles and clothing workshops for TRY 150 a week. Migrants receive only half or a third of the wages that local workers receive for the same job. Child labourers always work for less (Afanasieva, 2016).

The biggest complaint Syrian workers express concerns employers who do not pay their wages or who do not pay them on time. After being paid regularly for three-to-four months, they say that they start to receive very little money or, more commonly, none at all (Akdeniz, 2014: 23). They also work long hours. For example, Fatima, a Syrian woman living in Hatay, reported that her husband was fired from a restaurant where he had been working from eight o'clock in the morning until eleven at night because he asked for a two-hour break (Amnesty International, 2014).

Their main difficulty is that since there is no record of them working, they cannot claim any rights. For instance, they are unable to make any claim if they have a work-related accident or if they develop an occupational disease during the course of their employment, and they have little recourse if their employers do not pay their wages. This situation represents an extreme case of labour exploitation and leads to chaos. It is going to be difficult to stop Syrians, who are unable to use legal channels to claim their rights, from causing damage to the employer, workplace or work equipment. An incident of this kind occurred in a subcontracting workshop in the Çağlayan district of İstanbul. Thirty workers whose wages had not been paid for months took over the machines. However, the employer complained to the police, and the Syrian workers were charged with theft (Akdeniz, 2014).

Of the Syrian migrants interviewed in a survey conducted with 124 households covering 744 persons by the Support to Life Association in İstanbul in 2016, 64 per cent said that they earned a living by working for regular wages mostly in textiles, construction and service sectors, while 23 per cent said that they worked for a daily rate in service sectors (Support to Life, 2016). Interviewees from the Bağcılar district reported that since there were many factories and workshops in the district, most Syrians did heavy work in sectors like construction and textiles. It was also reported that they received low wages:

In textiles, Turks are paid TRY 1,500 (about USD 500) per month while Syrians are paid TRY 750 (about USD 250). In the construction sector, Turks are paid TRY 70-100 (about USD 23-33) per day and Syrians TRY 30-40 (about USD 10-13).

Syrian labour has been a rescue boat for labour-intensive sectors in Turkey and has helped these sectors lower their labour costs. The main characteristics of labour-intensive sectors are their constant goal of tapping into cheap labour pools, the source being internally displaced migrants from eastern Turkey, who were known as international irregular or undocumented migrants and now Syrian refugees. Thus, the informal labour market integration path for Syrians is built through informal, insecure and harsh working conditions with no guarantee for any payment. Agricultural work has been one of these informal integration paths where Syrian migrants are taking the lion's share in most casual jobs generated by the sector.

The competition of the poor: Downward pressure on wages

The seasonal agricultural work is one of the best sites to examine the effects of Syrian labour on wage levels in extensively informal and labour-intensive sectors. Syrian agricultural workers have recently been spotlighted because their presence has accelerated competition with other worker groups in seasonal agricultural production. Public opinion noting that Syrians cost domestic workers their jobs because they are willing to accept lower pay has grown and is voiced frequently. The media has often covered this angle as well. According to the 2014 study of the Support to Life Association, Syrian migrants have increased the labour supply for seasonal agricultural work, and as a result intra-class conflict has arisen between domestic and Syrian workers. Syrian migrant involvement in seasonal agricultural work has caused daily wages to stagnate and the amount of work available for each household to fall in comparison with previous years. Household income from seasonal agricultural work has consequently fallen. These changes not only deepen labour exploitation but also increase tensions among different groups of workers (Support to Life, 2014). In the Support to Life Association report, a domestic agricultural worker (male, thirty-five years old, father of four) speaks of the situation as follows:

Syrians came and our time is up. . . . Does Turkey not have poor of its own? The bosses like it because it's cheap. Last year [a Syrian worker] was showing [a field owner] a 20 lira [TRY] bill, implying he would work for that amount. The going daily wage was 40 liras. (Support to Life, 2014: 76)³

In general, as this worker notes, domestic migratory workers believe that Syrians are pulling down wages and taking away their jobs

The Report of the Parliamentary Research Commission Established for the Study of the Problems of Seasonal Agricultural Workers emphasizes similar issues (GNAT, 2015). It also states that wages have been pushed down by the involvement of Syrian migrant workers in particular.

> Employers see foreign workers as a store of cheap labour and employ them despite their lack of work permits. It has been observed that foreign nationals accept lower pay and harsher working conditions out of desperation. This situation leads to risks both in terms of labour markets and from the point of view of health and social problems, and constitutes a significant source of difficulties in service provision. (GNAT, 2015: 176)

With the inclusion of foreign migrant workers in seasonal agricultural labour, existing problems have become exacerbated, and it is possible that they will worsen in the future. Both reports underline the conflict and potential social tensions between foreign migrant workers and domestic workers. The rural antagonism between local populations and migrant workers from eastern Turkey has become more complex with the arrival of foreign migrant workers. The tension between domestic migrant seasonal agricultural workers and Syrian workers and the reactions of local populations towards both workers from south-eastern Turkey and Syrian workers are the most obvious reflection of the social change in Turkey on the labour market.

Syrian labour in Turkey's seasonal agricultural production

My research with Syrian agricultural workers involves two surveys in the province of Adana, where large-scale farming takes place year-round and produces a wide range of products for national and international markets. The first face-to-face survey, conducted in July 2016 in the tent settlements of seasonal workers living and working in the Adana Plain, covered a total of 1,662 individuals belonging to 266 Syrian households. This survey was one of the first large-scale surveys in the region, focusing on a specific group of Syrians engaged in agricultural work.

The research findings collected from these households reveal the striking character of Syrian agricultural families: 78 per cent of the sample migrated from a rural area of Syria. Their affinity for agricultural work and ability to endure life in tents is partly related to their rural background. Of all household members, 50.5 per cent are male and 49.5 per cent are female. This sex distribution points strongly to a pattern of migration of whole families. One of the most salient aspects of the typical flow of refugees towards Western Europe is that it consists of young male asylum seekers, while in Adana, the group studied migrated and continued to live as family units. While the average age of men representing the 266 households was 38.6, the average age of women was 32.2. For all household members (N: 1,662), the average age of men was 19.8 and the average age of women was 17.7. The sample was younger than the average for the Syrian population in Turkey, with 52.7 per cent of all household members consisting of those younger than eighteen. Only 15 per cent of the population was older than thirty. Approximately a quarter of the population was of the age of compulsory education. Low levels of education and illiteracy were common. Almost half of the group was illiterate, and the proportion of those who dropped out of primary education was 23.7 per cent. Only one-fifth of the total number of interviewees had completed a primary school education.

Syrians are registered under TP and special identity numbers beginning with the code number 99, *kimlik*, are issued to them in Turkey. *Kimlik* gives migrants the right to reside in Turkey, as well as access to basic health care and education; 88.4 per cent of the 1,662 individuals covered in the sample had a temporary protection *kimlik*, while 11.6 per cent were residing in Turkey without identification documents. It is not known whether this high ratio is unique to the sample, or what proportion of the total Syrian population in Turkey had registered. Half of the interviewees crossed the border with their spouses and children, while others were accompanied by members of their extended families. These findings are in keeping with other findings regarding forced mass migration, showing that families abandoned their homes en masse.

Decreasing numbers of native workers from nearby provinces had been increasing labour costs of Adana's agricultural producers. The arrival of Syrians remedied this situation; Syrians have begun to replace native-born labour in the region and have been instrumental in keeping costs competitive. This overlapped with labour shortages generated by workers from Şanlıurfa tending to stay in their home provinces for work, with the onset of irrigated agriculture in and around Şanlıurfa. Producers on the Adana Plain have used Syrian migrants to solve their labour supply problems and now have access to a greater workforce pool at a lower cost. Over the last few years, agricultural production in Adana has been carried out mainly by Syrians living in Adana rather than by local agricultural workers travelling from Şanlıurfa, Mardin and Adıyaman, as in the past (Figure 4.1).

Syrians who work in harsh conditions in seasonal agricultural work are further exploited due to lower wage levels and worse working conditions and, therefore, they are on the lowest rung of the seasonal agricultural worker hierarchy. The proportion of Syrian household members reported to be working as agricultural wage labourers was 45.4 per cent. Workers endure long working days, around eleven to twelve hours, as a result of nature-bound production. Products have to be picked on time with a tight deadline before they get spoilt. For example, cherries need to be picked before they get too ripe or cauliflowers need to be planted during September each year. These work

Figure 4.1 A group of Syrian workers planting cauliflower in Adana. Source: The Development Workshop Archive.

characteristics lead workers to spend the whole day in the fields, from sunrise to sunset. The time that workers spend getting to the fields is also an important factor in calculating how much of the day they spend in work-related activities. Workers spend, on average, between half an hour and an hour getting to the fields. Taking the return journey into account as well, this means that between one and two hours per day are spent in travelling to and from work.

Conclusions

The arrival of Syrian refugees has had a prominent effect on labour markets in Turkey. Most refugees have been absorbed into the country's large informal economy, which is characterized by poor working conditions and low wages. Agriculture is one of the major sectors hiring Syrian labour in high numbers, and it is a site of competition between different worker groups that push wage levels downwards. The Turkish labour market offers Syrian refugees' integration on informal terms at the bottom of the social strata. The Law on Work Permits for Foreigners under TP issued in 2016 has been too weak to protect the precarious labour market position of Syrians. Although the regulation is a positive step in protecting refugees and facilitating their access to formal employment, its actual outreach has so far been limited.

Drawing on research findings collected in the summer of 2016 in Adana, this chapter focused on Syrian refugees' agricultural work in Turkey as a case for studying Syrian labour market activities, precarious integration as a bottom-up integration strategy and the relationship between migration and labour markets in Turkey. It underscores the government's central legal and policy frameworks that provide Syrians with some citizenship rights while Syrians are simultaneously pushed into precarious employment due to the existing structural conditions of the Turkish labour market. The analysis emphasizes that the existing conditions of legal rights available to Syrians and the labour markets built up two different pathways of integration for Syrian refugees: formal and informal, with informal being the more common.

The present situation of Syrians in Turkey also presents the risk of a large population that has not benefitted sufficiently from education and other basic social rights and services, and lives in constant poverty and social exclusion. The migrant population in particular and segments of the local population who live beneath the poverty line have the potential to be locked into significant poverty. This could also be an indicator of future tension between different groups of people living under precarious conditions. As an already low-educated population has lost access to the formal education system through migration, their chances of breaking the cycle of poverty have become even slimmer. Keeping in mind the scarcity and even absence of financial resources to specifically income-generating activities of Syrian refugees in Turkey due to forced migration and the limitations of their temporary protection status, access to formal, better paid and permanent jobs seems as the only solution to mitigate this risk. However, such a causality makes this dilemma quite hard to resolve.

5

Intersecting vulnerabilities of the labour supply

Syrian women and children

The agricultural sector's hunger for labour has led to a cycle of workers coming from the most disadvantaged groups for seasonal work. This rotation of workers has been the main characteristic of seasonal agricultural work for many years. When the Syrian crisis broke out in 2011, many Syrians stepped in to compete for this work, creating competition among the precariat of hosting communities and Syrian refugees. To win this competition, Syrians have applied certain strategies that are based not only on accepting the lowest wages but also on using their most vulnerable labour force – women and children.

Intersecting vulnerabilities, pioneered through women and children, have been the main strategy of the Syrian community competing for seasonal work. This chapter focuses on how Syrian women and child labour is used in Turkey's seasonal agricultural production to produce low-cost crops that compete in international markets or support low wages of domestic consumers in many mega Turkish cities. In the first part, I analyse women's work and its connections to production and social reproduction. Women's labour is at the centre not only of Syrian families' survival strategies but also of the sustainability of agricultural production since their labour is essential for social reproduction of their families' labour that supply low-cost workers. The second part of the chapter turns to how both families and the agricultural sector depend on child labour to meet the needs of individual families and the labour market. It sheds light on how the Syrian community perceives children, offers reasons for their work, justifies children's income generation and supports their education. This analysis shows that intersecting vulnerabilities of women and child labour have been part of Syrians' successful negotiation process in agricultural labour markets as women and children bear an infinite capacity to easily surrender to patriarchal and capitalistic control imposed on their labour.

At the crossroad of productive work and social reproduction: Syrian women's work and labour

The organization of the seasonal agricultural workforce intrinsically results in the overlapping of productive and reproductive work and shows that their connectedness is at the heart of seasonal work, which cannot be analysed without considering women's work and the patriarchal system underlying it. Moving all members of a family together to work is the strongest indication of how worker families rely on the interconnectedness of productive and reproductive work to gain access to income-earning potential in the agricultural sector, mostly through immeasurable use of women labour. Productive work in agriculture is only possible because of the work women perform in the realm of reproductive work, which systematically subsidizes capital and enables ultra-exploitation of migrant labour. Therefore, an analysis of the precarization of refugee labour is considerably determined not only under the impact of intensification and/or informalization of productive work but also in the ways social reproduction internalizes production costs to workers, families and communities, in this case Syrians. This part of the chapter first focuses on women's work in seasonal agricultural work, shaped under the auspice of patriarchal and capitalist exploitative relations, and then on social reproduction where neither employers nor the state bear any of the costs for socially reproducing labour; everything is dumped onto the shoulders of refugee women.

The realm of production

Patriarchy, the rule of the father and older male authority figures over women/girls and younger men/boys, is the fundamental basis for women's subordination as well as male control over women's labour and reproductive capacity (Cockburn, 1991; Bradley, 1996). Enmeshing patriarchal relations with market forces has affected women's labour market activities, and feminist analysts have regarded labour markets as 'bearers of gender' (Elson, 1999: 611).

The world of work has been the bearer of gendered hierarchies and a gendered division of labour in employment. Patriarchal structures in culture, society, markets and corporations have kept women within the confines of particular activities in the informal economy, thereby hindering women's financial and social gains through their paid work (Mies, 1982; Beneria and Roldan, 1987; Carr and Alter Chen, 2002; Heintz, 2006). Even when women increasingly enter into paid work, they frequently engage in the lowest-paid, highly precarious jobs (Chen et al., 2005). Seasonal agricultural work is one of the precarious sectors where women are frequently used as a source of cheap and vulnerable labour. Migrant women's role in agricultural production has been the topic of earlier studies that emphasize women's double burden and display the interconnectedness of the realms of production and social reproduction (Preibisch and Encalada Grez, 2010; Dolan, 2005; Nieto, 2014).

Syrian refugee women have been the most recent addition to the agricultural labour force in Turkey and a major supply-side strategy used by Syrians to compete for agricultural jobs. Of the 112 Syrian households (N = 905) I surveyed in the tent settlements in Adana in 2017, 56 per cent of the women/girls are engaged in agricultural work (254 out of 453 women), whereas men's/boys' rate of agricultural work is 64 per cent. Figure 5.1 illustrates the relationship between age groups and agricultural work and the high participation rate of young girls and boys. The rate for girls aged six to

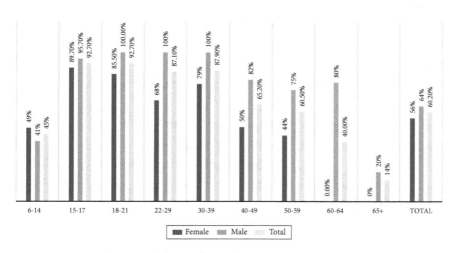

Figure 5.1 Agriculture work by gender and age groups (N = 905). Source: The 2017 Survey Findings.

fourteen is 49.3 per cent and increases to 89.7 per cent for girls aged fifteen to seventeen. Girls tend to work in high numbers until the age of marriage.

The rate of women's agricultural work among the Syrians surveyed is much higher than women's overall labour market participation for both Syrian and Turkish women. One of the most recent reports on Syrian women living in Turkey published by UN Women and ASAM (Association for Solidarity with Asylum Seekers and Migrants) in 2018 presents findings from surveys and interviews with 1,291 Syrian women and girls in 7 provinces and shows that 15 per cent of the sample group were working in permanent or temporary/seasonal jobs in agriculture, textile and service sectors (UNWOMEN-ASAM, 2018: 8–45). The Centre for Transnational Development and Collaboration (CTDC, 2015: 10), for example, states that 'According to UN data, women's labour force participation in Syria was 13% in 2010. Currently 17% of the Syrian women living in Turkey are in the labour force' (CTDC, 2015: 9–10). The report also notes that

> with restrictions on Syrian refugees' employment in Turkey . . ., the burden is even heavier for women heads of households trying to secure a living for themselves and their household members. . . . For women, low access to work is similar to that of men; however, women often find themselves engaging in income-generating activities such as petty trading, seasonal agricultural work and cleaning. (CTDC, 2015: 9–10)

The presence of a high number of Syrian women in Turkey's agricultural sector reflects the feminization of agricultural production. Earlier arguments (Çınar, 2014) have pointed out that the feminization of the seasonal agricultural workforce is the result of patriarchal control exercised over women and women's dependent role on the hierarchical chain of paternal relations. In this setting, women generally take part in agricultural work not as individuals but as an extension of their family or household (Çınar, 2014: 181). Feminization is visible in the number of women who work in agriculture and in the discourses of who is the best worker. It is often emphasized that agriculture is women's work. A *dayıbaşı* in Adana (fifty-three years old, twenty years of experience), for example, explained how he forms his worker teams, showing preference for female workers:

> Everyone knows that women are the main workers. When forming our worker teams, we always seek to have women. Otherwise when there are no

women, no work gets done at all. They work hard and fast. They are diligent at what they do.... Young men can be troublemakers from time to time but women and girls are easily controlled!

As this labour intermediary noted, women were perceived as ideal workers because of their hard work ethic and the ease with which they could be managed.

Syrian women continuously maintained that their lives back in Syria had been radically different. For example, a mother of five discussed her changing work pattern and roles:

Back in Syria, only men worked and one income was enough to support a family. My husband was a butcher and we had a small plot of land in the village we lived in. I used to do the work in our garden and look after my family.... Here we have to work all family together but it is still not enough to support us. Men, women, boys and girls all work!

Women's changing working pattern from unpaid family workers to wage workers is perceived to be the result of forced migration and loss of the economic resources they used to have in Syria. Women verbalized their situation as an obligation (*mecbur*) to work. 'Look at us. I have to feed 9 people in my family. We arrived in Turkey with nothing, only the clothes on us.... The choice we have is hunger or work. We choose to work.... Mecbur, mecbur.' Working for pay after their passage to Turkey is a new situation for women. Working for an employee, meeting daily targets of harvesting/hoeing, being part of a work team and working for a specific length of time each day are all new routines for many Syrian refugee women.

Sending young girls into fields is also a new experience and a way for forming intersecting vulnerabilities from the most submissive labour of women and children. A mother (forty-five years old, six children) explained that her daughter has been working since the age of twelve:

Dilan is a very clever girl. Since we arrived here and live with Turkish and Kurdish workers she has learnt both languages. Quick learner. We couldn't afford to send her to school. She now works in the fields together with her brothers. I know it is hard work but we are helpless and have no other way to turn to.

Young girls are the ideal workers for *dayıbaşı* and farmers and great helpers for their mothers. In many cases, their labour is utilized since the early ages in the fields and in the tent settlements.

The inclusion of Syrian women and girls into seasonal agriculture has led the way to build a 'multiplication of labour' and 'differential inclusion of migrants' (Mezzadra and Neilson, 2013) in Turkish agricultural labour markets. The role of migratory movements in regulating labour markets is limited to not only the diversification of labour sources but also the extent of the intensification of labour exploitation and deterioration of working conditions. Syrian refugees – men, women, children, sometimes even those who are pregnant or have disabilities – endure harsh working conditions and long working hours. Otherwise, the risk of falling beneath the subsistence level is a big threat (Figure 5.2).

Female agricultural workers endure harsh working conditions. In an interview, a group of female orange pickers in Adana, Fatma, twenty-five years old, mother of two children, expressed their working conditions:

> Our day starts quite early. We wake up around 4.00 am in the morning. Because we need to finish our work around 2.00 or 3.00 pm in the afternoon.... We go to the orange fields on an old vehicle, almost 50 years old, in great discomfort. It may take from 30 minutes to 45 minutes to reach the gardens.... As soon as we arrive, we start working immediately. No

Figure 5.2 A group of women workers in Adana. Source: Development Workshop Archive.

time to slow down and rest as the *çavuş* (foreman) keeps shouting out loud, 'hurry', 'come on', 'do not slow down'.

A usual workday lasts almost twelve hours, basically from dawn to sunset. In Turkey, there is long-hour work culture, especially in the informal sector, with weekly working hours usually exceeding the legal forty-eight-hour limit.[1]

What makes long work hours more unusual in agriculture is the harsh environment and climate in which the work takes place. Workers are exposed to extreme weather conditions (extreme heat, cold, wind and precipitation) and undertake physically demanding tasks involving ergonomic hazards, such as bending over and repetitive movements. A young mother of two reported their working conditions:

> This is Adana you know. It is almost 50 degrees under the sun. You have to bend all day long to pick peppers. When peppers are hot, the weather is hot, I feel like from time to time I will go crazy at one point. It is really hard to bear the conditions. We stay in the field all day long. Mecbur!

On one of my site visits, I came across a team of six, men and women, planting cauliflowers. They were bending down to plant little branches while standing up in watery mud up to their knees. Although it was mid-October when the weather was mild and not too cold, standing in mud for twelve hours per day is challenging and threatening to one's health. A young woman planting cauliflower in the field said:

> Do you see how we work all day long? We are wet up to our knees. Probably we will get sick soon. Then who will work for our families? What we do is impossible working conditions for anyone. . . . We work in this condition almost 10 hours daily.

Extreme hot or cold weather, slippery and wet surfaces, isolated fields with no water and sanitary facilities, the risk of flooding and insect bites are all dangers facing workers (Figure 5.3).

What makes these conditions more challenging for Syrian women is that most of these women had never worked as wage workers before. Some women from rural backgrounds in Syria were familiar with agricultural work, but for most, working in agriculture is a post-migration experience.

Hard-working conditions do not bring women a high-earning potential but only subsistence wages. In October 2017, workers in the Adana province

Figure 5.3 Syrian women workers in Adana's fields. Source: Development Workshop Archive.

earned TRY 55 for their daily work and paid around 10 per cent commission to their labour intermediary. In 2017, if a worker earned around twenty-five days of wages in a month, their total earnings were less than the monthly minimum wage.[2]

Given the wage levels in Adana, Turkish workers blame Syrian workers for the low level of earnings in daily farm work. A Turkish woman, thirty-five years old and mother of six, complained about the Syrians and their effect on wages in agriculture:

> Before Syrians arrived, I was making TRY 65 a day. But today, because of them, because there are a lot of workers fighting for the same job, I work for TRY 55. . . . My living expenses are increasing but my earnings are decreasing. This is not fair. . . . My family and I will not come to Adana to work again. We will move to central Anatolia, to work in the sugar beet fields. . . . Syrians endangered my bread!

Competition for existing jobs between Syrian and Turkish workers mostly results in decreasing their wages but increasing the profits of farm owners and traders. Decreasing workers' wages, however, means that workers have to work longer hours and more members of a family have to work to meet a family's subsistence level. In a work regime where workers are already working up to their physical limits, the only strategy is to draw on the labour of almost all family members as much as possible. A young girl aged eighteen years tells her situation:

> I would have never worked if we were back in Syria. Only my father would go to work. Here life is so expensive and we have nothing here. We all have to work. My brother who is 12 years old started to go to the field this year. We all need to work. My father has a heart condition and is too old to work in a field.

Another reason for a high number of Syrian women in seasonal agricultural work is the control exercised over them at work. Women often reported that their every move is under strict observation and control. Whether they are allowed to talk to each other while working, how many rows they have to finish, when and where they take breaks and so on are always subject to orders and/or permission. The performance system also works as a form of discipline and control. Some of the workers told me that the *çavuş* (foreman) constantly monitors their performance and every move. Fatma, my informant, explains the control exercised over them at work:

> Here I'm working in packaging the picked oranges into these boxes which are taken to bazaars all over Turkey and sold. You see as well he stands over me and watches how I work very closely. I cannot even slow down a little bit. He keeps shouting out, 'come on, come on'!

In labour studies research, workers' speed is considered fast when they are aligning with machines at which they work. In labour-intensive sectors, such as agriculture, workers' work pattern is set with other measures, such as the number of oranges picked by a team or the number of sacks filled with peppers. Therefore, work speed is set by a foreman, whose authority over women and girls is more powerful than over men and boys. Men's power to discipline workers is the main reason for employing women and children in seasonal farm work.

Women are preferred as workers not only because of their hard work and 'God-given' skills for agricultural work but also because of the degree of control that can be exercised over their labour and income. The diffusion of patriarchal control over women's labour and earnings is related to family-based worker teams, where women work together with other close family members and relatives. Male heads of households and *dayıbaşı*s form an alliance to decide who works from a specific family. Their collaboration also extends to controlling the income generated. Thus, women's earnings are directly paid to male heads of households, mostly their fathers or husbands. As a result, women depend on their fathers or husbands for their personal needs and expenses. Women are never paid the wages they earn and do not have control over their cash income. A middle-aged mother, working with her three children in orange fields, expressed the situation in the following statement:

> All the money we make is paid to my husband. He is not working but he is the one making deals with the labour intermediary and receives the payment. They together decide how many people will go to work on a specific day and how much the wage will be. Then, of course, our wages are paid to him. We do not even know how much we make from the work we do. For example, we pick oranges for two weeks for an employer but do not know how much our total earning is.

Patriarchal ideologies diffused into seasonal agricultural work practices dictate where and how women should work and extract the fruits of women's labour. This patriarchal alliance might be called a *masculine aura* that facilitates the perpetuation of patriarchal control over the labour of women and children and reproduces existing gender-based hegemonies. The earnings of children and women are not only seized but also made into instruments for the continuation of patriarchal hegemony. The basic dynamics of patriarchal relations are preserved, even when males do not have any earning potential themselves nor contribute to household income at all.

Syrian women's work in Turkey's seasonal agricultural work is one way the refugee community builds its main survival strategy. After migration to Turkey, more and more Syrian women entered wage work in agriculture to help their families secure their livelihoods by generating a highly insecure and precarious workforce. However, women contribute to the precarization of Syrians through their activities in not only the productive realm but also in the realm of social reproduction where women play a significant role. The next section focuses on the social reproduction of the agricultural labour force.

The realm of social reproduction

The old debate about housework in feminist literature has been revitalized in recent years to incorporate the role of social reproduction in the precarization of labour on the global scale (Mezzadri, 2020). The focus is on 'how realms of social reproduction co-constitute the dynamics of exploitation observed in production, as they co-produce the key processes necessary to extract labour surplus from labouring masses, and hence co-participate to the overall generation of (surplus) value'. (Mezzadri, 2020: 157). In a seminal study, Maria Mies has pointed to the tight connection between production and social reproduction among lace makers in India; women produced intricate laces for the world market from their peri-urban and rural homes. Mies explores the features of housewifization as a process of the devaluation of women's reproductive labour inside the household. The very nature of women's reproductive labour sets the basis for their disadvantage in paid employment outside the home and through which women connect to global capitalism. Also, the masterful gendered analysis of labour indenture by Gaiutra Bahadur (2014) highlights the violent appropriation of women's labour across productive and reproductive domains at work on US plantations in the late nineteenth century, which not only devalued but also objectified women both at work and at home.

Women's activities taking place in the realm of social reproduction are as vital to seasonal agricultural work as the activities done in the fields and on farms. Worker families' movement from one province to another, carrying all their household possessions to construct a home in a tent camp, results in the mobilization of women's reproductive labour to care for families and, at the same time, the release of that labour for work in the fields. The work of women in the realm of social reproduction also enables workers to survive with lower wage levels.

Migrant women face a double burden of agricultural production and domestic responsibilities at home. The intensification of women's workload is the result of deteriorating living conditions and longer wage work time (Hennebry, 2014). The migration process has increased not only the time women spend on agricultural production but also the time they spend on domestic chores and caring activities. This is mostly due to living in a tent settlement. Migrant women have to spend more time and exert greater effort to reorganize life in temporary and non-standard shelters and devote more time for the care needs of family members and for other household chores. The heavy burden shouldered by women in harsher living conditions results in a division of labour between different female members of families, as the younger ones do agricultural work and the older ones stay at home and do domestic tasks.

Living in tent camps that are pitched on bare ground in open air and usually made of nylon with no access to refrigeration, running water and electricity makes the tasks women undertake even harder. A Syrian woman (thirty years old and mother of five children) described her living conditions:

> We used to have a nice house with a garden. Now, look at us, we live in this dust and mud. I have to carry water to cook and other things. . . . It is really difficult to adapt. It is really difficult to protect ourselves from all sorts of dangers such as floods, insects, snakes.

All household activities – like cooking, doing laundry, taking care of children, gathering wood for fuel, carrying water and taking care of oneself and ensuring basic hygiene – are more exhausting and take more time under these conditions.

The burden of these responsibilities falls unevenly on the shoulders of women and girls. Women are solely responsible for housework and caring activities without any help from men. The survey that took place in Adana in 2016 reveals gender disparities in domestic activities in which women undertake the following activities disproportionately: doing laundry (97.7 per cent), washing dishes (96 per cent), cooking (98 per cent), cleaning (95.1 per cent) and taking care of the elderly (48.5 per cent). Girls partner with their mothers in doing all these activities. Domestic work is seen to be a part of girls' socialization process and prepares them to be sole providers of these services in their own future homes. Men only take up just a few household activities, such as carrying water (62.4 per cent) and managing the family budget and shopping (89.1 per cent), for example. When there is a need to go into the public realm and contact the outside world, such as when children need to visit the hospital, usually both parents attend with their children (43.2 per cent). However, when only one of the parents goes, it is usually the father (33.1 per cent) rather than the mother (15 per cent). A woman's contact with the outside world is generally avoided and is frowned upon (Figure 5.4).

Figure 5.4 A woman cooking for her children near her tent. Source: Development Workshop Archive.

The women or the girls in the house take care of younger children, the elderly and the disabled. Among the Syrian agricultural worker families in Adana, childcare responsibilities fall almost solely on women (96.2 per cent). The fertility rate is relatively high among these families and almost all adults go to work in the fields during the day, leaving the children to take care of each other most of the time. Elderly care, on the other hand, is a problematic issue for these families; 32.7 per cent of the households have an elderly member who needs care, according to the survey. Once again, it is women who provide care services to these elders.

Women's days start quite early in tent settlements whether they prepare to go to work or not. Preparing breakfast, lunch and dinner takes quite a long time and energy as workers bring their meals to work. Bread is the main staple for Syrians, as well as Turks, and Syrian women cook their own bread, creating a lot of work for women already living under difficult domestic arrangements. In Turkish society, bread is usually bought from bakeries or small shops selling essential food and drinks (*bakkal*); women no longer cook bread at home. However, Turkish and Syrian women alike in agricultural worker families bake bread for all meals, which is a time-consuming task but essential for their survival. The food brought to work prepared by women is the main energy source that workers rely on. During tea or lunch breaks, they eat whatever they bring with them. One can imagine how a woman living in a house of eight people is busy preparing bread, cooking meals, cleaning and caring for others.

During one of my fieldwork visits in Şanlıurfa, I visited a group of workers picking cotton under the hot sun of early September. The temperature was over 40° C. A group of three families, mostly composed of children in their early teens, were picking cotton in a large cotton field. Towards mid-day, the mother of five children, Nahide, prepared lunch for the workers under the rundown shed of a tractor. The lunch was composed of a loaf of a bread, a couple of slices of tomatoes and cucumbers and a small amount of cooked peppers. It could have been the first meal of the day not only for the adults but also for the children. I was too ashamed to ask. Nahide explained what she did for her family in the following words:

> I wake up around 4.00 am to prepare the meals we eat during the day working in the field (*tarla*). You know that we make our own bread almost every other day. I pack everything before everybody wakes up. Then, we go to the field to pick cotton. We need to preserve our food because keeping the food unspoiled is a challenge under the hot sun in Urfa. . . . When we get back, I put the fire on to cook and clean. It is almost 11 or 12 before I go to bed.

Nahide brought three of her children with her to the field. The youngest was nine and picked cotton. Fatma was the same age as my daughter who went back to her school in the early days of September, but Fatma was too busy working and unable to attend school in Turkey.

In tent camps, children are often looked after by no one and run around from morning to evening. They create their own games and their own toys. Whatever attracts their attention around the site becomes their toy. Care is considered to be providing food for the children most of the time. It is a bit different with newborns, but as soon as a child can walk, they become the communal child of the tent site. There is no shortage of peers, as there are lots of children of all ages. Caring for newborn babies is important and demands the attention of mothers. In some cases, mothers take their babies to fields with them. As soon as a child reaches the toddler stage, they can be left in the care of other children. Eight- or ten-year-old girls go around with babies in their laps and they are considered an adult when they reach the age of twelve or thirteen.

It is common to see children looking after toddlers and spending time with them in worker tent camps all over Turkey. Nahide explained that she leaves her youngest children in the tent area without any adult supervision.

> When I go to work, I leave them in the care of the oldest who is only 8 years old. She is responsible for her two younger brothers. There are also elders in other tents; they also watch over my children.

The number of children usually outnumbers adults in these camps where children caring for babies, toddlers and their younger siblings raise the next generation of the precariat for agricultural work. Seeing children walking around barefoot on stony ground difficult to walk on even in boots or carrying water buckets heavier than themselves is a strong indicator of how social reproductive activities co-constitute productive work in modern capitalism.

The workload of women who live in tents and participate in agricultural production is much heavier than those women living in proper dwellings. Women live in tent settlements that do not have running water or adequate kitchen and bathroom facilities and equipment, and are devoid of the benefits of electricity. Accordingly, they find such activities as cooking and baking bread, washing dishes and laundry and caring for their children and meeting their sanitary needs very tiring and time consuming. To do laundry, they have to carry water, which is warmed up by collected firewood. The burden of these activities falls disproportionately on the shoulders of women and girls.

The domestic distribution of labour between men and women also shows that women are generally engaged in traditional housework and childcare activities. Washing laundry and dishes, cooking, baking bread, cleaning and taking care of the elderly are generally tasks carried out by women. In seasonal agricultural worker families, women take on a double burden. They work in the fields and perform these household activities. Men, on the other hand, are more active in the public activities of the household. For example, shopping, and in some cases taking children to the hospital are tasks performed by men. Men serve as liaisons with agricultural intermediaries, the neighbourhood foremen (*muhtar*) and other individuals from the local community. Financial matters are under the jurisdiction of men; women depend on men in public and economic matters.

Gender and marriage

The precaritization of Syrian women's work embedded in patriarchal relations is enforced through the practice of marriage, which has implications for migration and women's legal and matrimonial status in the Syrian community. Marriage is significant in young women's transition from childhood to adulthood. Through marriage, they become the bearers of a patriarchal set of values and are responsible for passing these values onto future generations. These duties are performed via their positions as wives and mothers. Women's status in their families and communities is defined by motherhood and wifehood.

According to the data collected in 2017 in the province of Adana (N = 905), women's marital status is a vital factor that affects their standing in both their families and the labour market: 59.9 per cent of Syrian migrant women in Adana were single due to their young age, while 37 per cent were currently married. Marrying young is also quite common in this Syrian community: 23.7 per cent of women between the ages of fifteen and seventeen were married, and 50.8 per cent of women between eighteen and twenty-one were married. When asked how coming to Turkey affected the average marriage age, most stated that there was no impact at all and that both males and females reaching age fifteen were viewed as nubile. Survey answers reveal that no significant changes had occurred in the marrying ages of women due to migration. When Syrian women are asked about the ideal age to marry, the reply usually was 'whenever fate allows it to be' (Figure 5.5).

Some interesting variations regarding marriage practices were observed among Syrian women coming from different ethnic and cultural backgrounds. In some groups, marrying before the age of twenty was rare and deemed to be imprudent, while other groups encouraged marriage after the age of fifteen. For example, families with rural backgrounds and ties desired to keep similar practices of marriage as it was in Syria and encouraged only group marriages.

Syrians I interviewed during my fieldwork considered that the marriage affairs can be a risky endeavour since migration may increase the probability of family units falling apart (Nawa, 2017); no such attitude or motivation was detected among the Syrian migrants in Adana. Traditional wedding ceremonies

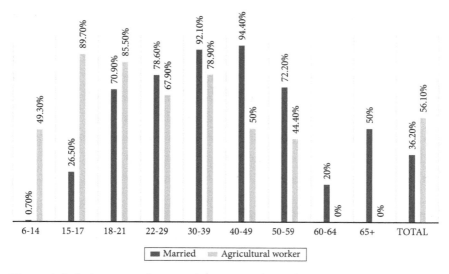

Figure 5.5 Syrian women's marital statues and employment. Source: The 2017 Survey Findings.

and dowry traditions continue uninterrupted. Interviewees claimed that the wedding ceremonies held in Syria were lively with more guests attending, and dowries were more generous and incomparable to the ones they had in Turkey. However, due to economic difficulties, the dowries prepared in Turkey could only include bare essentials. Migrant families in general avoided purchasing expensive durable household items for newly married couples, such as furniture and appliances, since they may one day have to leave them behind in Turkey when the family returns to Syria. The bride's family is generally paid TRY 4,000–5,000 by the groom's family. Similar to practices in Turkey, newlyweds usually live with the groom's family and the lineage continues through patriarchal channels. Marriage between Turkish males and Syrian females is generally discouraged for fear that when families return to Syria, these women are likely to stay behind with their Turkish husbands. To avoid these situations, Syrian girls are sometimes forced to marry Syrian males in a hurried fashion. Furthermore, male polygamy (*kumalık*) is quite common.

Civil (officially registered) marriages have become non-existent among migrants; this is perhaps the most striking transitory impact of marriage practices following mass migration. Syrian women stated that a common practice in Syria used to be marrying with a religious ceremony and applying for a family registry booklet, an official register in which all members of a family are recorded, making the nuptials official. Registering a marriage guarantees the woman rights to file for a divorce, to demand alimony and child support and to sue for custody of her children. Even though marriages among migrants in Turkey can be registered through the General Directorate of Migration Management, no such applications were reported by the households surveyed in Adana. The end result is a serious deprivation of women's legal protection and rights regarding marriage. Without any legal rights, women's position inside the family is dictated solely by patriarchal customs and values, leaving their fate in the hands of the male-dominant society.

Gendered implications of migration

The migration process generally induces changes in migrant women's position within their families and traditional gender relations. For some women, migration may mean an increase in social mobility, economic independence and relative autonomy. Theoretically, migration may improve women's empowerment and social position if it leads to increased participation in employment, more control over earnings and greater participation in family decision-making (Pessar, 1984). New economic and social responsibilities may change the distribution of power within the family, leading to greater authority and participation in household decision-making and control over the family's resources. Positive shifts may result in the relationship between immigrant women and their husbands and children. Alternatively, migration may leave gender asymmetries largely unchanged even though certain dimensions of gender inequalities are modified (Espiritu, 2005). The second aspect of status change discussed in the literature on women and migration focuses on the impact of moving from one form of gender stratification system to another. In general terms, this means moving from one system of patriarchy to another.

Analysing changes in gender relations is challenging and needs to be framed within analytical categories. Thus, transformations in gender relations after the migration process can be evaluated using the framework of Elson and Pearson (1981), who conceptualize the impact of social change and female employment on gender subordination in terms of tendencies to decompose and intensify existing forms of gender subordination and to recompose new forms of subordination. The decomposition of gender subordination may be seen in the status and power that immigration to Turkey brings to women, both at home and in their community. Furthermore, 'work enhances women's self-esteem as wives and mothers, affords them income to actualize these roles more fully and provides them with a heightened leverage to participate equally with men in household decision making' (Pessar, 1986: 281). As shown in the case of Syrian women in seasonal work, Syrian women started to take part in income-generating activities more than ever and recorded a high level of participation in paid work. It is possible that women have discovered their income-generating power for the first time and have silently gained greater power in their family and community. In an interview, Ferya (thirty-three years old and mother of four boys) explained the situation:

> It is really difficult to survive in Turkey. We had not known how to earn money before we came here. Only one earner was enough to look after a family in Syria but here that is not possible. We all have to work and women all started to work in fields. . . . It is true that we work for our families and men control all income, but I also see how women are coming to realize that they can make money as well.

Women finding a sense of newfound value in work has silently acknowledged their new role in income generation.

In Syrian households, women gain authority with age, which complies with the classic patriarchy model in which women exercise a considerable amount of power over younger household members. However, again, emerging opportunities for agricultural work and economic pressures to generate extra income always need to be balanced with women's traditional roles, which ultimately affect the meaning and value attached to their work.

The recomposition of gender subordination is seen in the consolidation of women's roles as mothers and wives in the social production. In the case of Syrian women, the recomposition of gender subordination can be observed in the intensification of their role – unpaid activities directly linked to paid activities have paved the way for cheaper food production, as explained by one of my female respondents (twenty-seven years old, three children, widow, living with her in-laws):

> Let's imagine how a family could survive in this deserted area if there are no women. Who would cook, clean and care? I work as hard as a worker in the field. I have to prepare breakfast and pack lunch for the workers of my family before they leave for work. . . . All day, I make bread, wash clothes and look after my babies and prepare for dinner before my workers arrive in the

evening. . . . Tell me who works harder me or the workers in the field and how we would have survived without all these.

The intensification of gender subordination of Syrian migrant women is observed in the increasing patriarchal control over women's work and public nature of that control. Even though the time women spend on paid and unpaid work has increased greatly after migrating to Turkey, their labour is taken captive by both the patriarchal and the capitalistic relations operating in their communities and the labour market. The result is that women expect little control over their income or labour. Their wages are viewed as family income and seized by the male head of the household. Besides their wages, their labour is also controlled by the male-dominated organization of agricultural work. The imposition of patriarchal control over women's labour and earnings is mostly the result of how agricultural work is managed and controlled by a group of men who form a patriarchal alliance: the male heads of households, labour intermediaries and landowners. For example, the decision of who will work in a given family is made by male family heads and labour intermediaries. Even if adult men are not working and the livelihood of the household is provided by women and children, the matter of how many and which individuals from a household work is decided in settings where men come together. Furthermore, intermediaries pay wages directly to heads of households, not to the female or child workers. Women's labour is the indiscernible piece of the negotiation process between the male heads of households, male labour intermediaries and male landowners. Patriarchal solidarity between men controls women's work and demands submission and docility when men grab the fruits of women's labour. This union of powers forged between men over work arrangements and wage payments creates a 'masculine aura' and maintains patriarchal control over women and children. Through networks from which women and children are completely excluded, the labour of women and children is seized and made an instrument of the continuity of male dominance.

Precarization and Syrian child labour in Turkey's agricultural sector

The intersecting vulnerabilities embedded in child labour in Turkey's agricultural sector are used to win the competition among the poor for access to agricultural work. Deploying child labour in farm work is not unique to Syrian refugees but a long-lasting practice in the world of waged work in agricultural where seasonal worker families, whether Turkish, Kurdish or Arab, and farmers utilize child workers in high numbers. With the entrance of Syrians into seasonal farm work, the situation has only intensified, which was, before, a policy battlefield for policymakers, nongovernmental organizations (NGOs) and international groups. To make matters worse, Turkey became a signatory to the ILO Convention 182, Worst Forms of Child Labour in 2001, to eliminate the worst forms of child labour in Turkey. In Turkey's national plan, seasonal migratory agricultural work is accepted to be the worst form of child labour and to be eliminated for children aged under eighteen years. The Syrian refugee flow, however, has exacerbated the abuse of child labour and made it more difficult to implement policy solutions due to its highly informal and fragmented nature.

This section examines the role of Syrian child labour in seasonal agricultural work and child labour as a path to precarization. This part focuses on the extent of child labour in Syrian households, the perceptions on child labour and the justifications for child labour by families, labour intermediaries and farmers. By and large, it shows that children's work in agriculture is instrumental for families to ensure survival and for farmers to tap into cheap labour forms. Syrian child workers have emerged as the new precariat of Turkey and have heavily engaged in informal jobs in mostly labour-intensive sectors ranging from construction to textiles and agriculture with no other prospect in education and alternative decent job opportunities. In agriculture, they are mostly stuck in destitute situations under difficult conditions and have a very slim chance of breaking away from hard agricultural labour.

The role of child labour in seasonal agricultural production

Turkey has policies in place legally restricting child labour. Article 71 of Turkish Labour Law 4857 forbids the employment of children under the age of fifteen, with the exception of children aged fourteen and up who have completed compulsory education and are hired for light duties that do not intervene with their education and physical, psychological and social development.[3] Children's employment in agricultural production is further regulated by other special rules. For example, the ILO Convention 182 states that the minimum age of employment in agricultural production is sixteen. The Turkish Ministry of Family, Labour and Social Services (formerly Labour and Social Security) prepared the Second National Plan Against Child Labour in accordance with the ILO Convention 182 in 2017. According to the plan, the worst forms of child labour in Turkey are 'working on the street', 'working in small- and medium-scale enterprises doing heavy and dangerous tasks' and 'paid seasonal and migrant work in agriculture, outside family enterprises'. The programme aims to prevent seasonal agricultural employment of children by covering all health and education needs of children who migrate with their families (Çalışma ve Sosyal Güvenlik Bakanlığı, 2017).

Even though Turkey has legal regulations for child labour, child work is prevalent, especially in the informal agriculture sector. The state of child work in seasonal agricultural production has been a focus of policymakers, academics and human rights activists for many years, and various studies present high numbers of children working in agriculture and important findings regarding their working and living conditions. Out of all working children in 2012, 44.7 per cent were employed in agricultural production,[4] primarily of citrus fruits, cotton, tobacco, cumin and hazelnuts. A recent report by the Grand National Assembly of Turkey estimated that one-third of one million people in Turkey employed in seasonal agricultural work were children (GNAT, 2015). Those between the ages of fourteen and seventeen comprise the prime workforce of seasonal work in agriculture and are engaged in the production of many crops in different regions of Turkey. The 2014 Support to Life Association study, which covered 168 seasonal agricultural worker households and gathered data on 1,353 individuals, shows that 35 per cent of 5–11-year-old children worked in fields, while the rate is 78 per cent for 12–15-year-olds and 85 per cent for 16–18-year-olds. A similar finding (Development Workshop, 2014) reveals heavy engagement of child workers in the hazelnut harvest in the western Black Sea region.[5]

Many studies focusing on the working conditions of children reveal that children work as long and as hard as adults in agriculture (Support to Life, 2014; Development Worksop, 2014; Semerci and Erdoğan, 2017; FLA, 2017). For example, a study conducted by the Development Workshop (2014) shows that in hazelnut harvesting, the usual working day starts for all at 7.00 am and stops at 7.00 pm and during the twelve-hour workday, workers are only allowed to benefit from ninety minutes of break time, which they can use for meals or rest. Since children are not physically full developed, enduring these conditions and long working days have the worst effect on them. Children not only work for crop harvesting but also carry plastic bins and bags full of hazelnuts that may weigh more than 20 kilograms. The Development Workshop report shows that children enter the workforce with the consent of their families, labour intermediaries and farmers. In fact, in their negotiations for work in the hazelnut harvest, families often demand that their children also be given work by the employers. The economic needs of the families are given as the primary reason for integrating children into harvest work. Worker families bring along their children with the motivation of increasing their income, as more people working results in more money (Semerci and Erdoğan, 2017). Children are assets to families not only by earning money but also by taking some women's burden off their shoulders. They undertake the tasks of carrying water, washing clothes, cleaning up tents, making beds, washing dishes, preparing meals, setting tables and caring for younger children.

Living conditions in tent settlements have certain risks and dangers for children's well-being. Tent and worksites pose a series of particular risks and threats (Semerci and Erdoğan, 2017). Usually, there is no clean drinking water, proper electrical wiring or hygienic toilet and bathroom facilities in tent settlements. These settlements, generally established along roads or canals, do not offer proper protection from intemperate climate conditions or from insect and snake bites and do not provide access to health-care services. Furthermore, in farm work, children constantly repeat the same set of motions, leading to ergonomic problems and a negative impact on their physical development (Figure 5.6).

Seasonal work has a devastating impact on children's educational attainment. The 2014 Support to Life Association's study focusing on Turkish seasonal agricultural workers shows that child agricultural workers drop out of school or are absent regularly throughout the year. In fact, 50 per cent of children (eighteen and under) actively engaged in seasonal work left school altogether, while the 57 per cent of child workers who continue their education do not attend school regularly. Work in seasonal agricultural production hinders children's education and increases their risk of dropping out.

Adding to the earlier concerns of child workers in general, Syrian children's participation has worsened the situation of child labour in agriculture. Child labour is used as the main survival strategy of Syrian families living throughout

Figure 5.6 Children packing onions. Source: Development Workshop Archive.

Turkey. Many children are engaged in informal work in many sectors, such as textiles, construction, footwear and solid waste collection in urban areas. According to Ayhan Kaya and Aysu Kirac (2016), at least one child works in almost every third Syrian household in Istanbul. Labour has been a part of daily life for many Syrian children, and it is not exclusive to the agricultural sector.

The number of child workers has increased with Syrians' participation in seasonal agricultural work. My 2017 fieldwork reveals that children between the ages of six and seventeen account for 46 per cent of all workers in the sample. The rate of working children in the same age group is 60.9 per cent. Children between six and fourteen make up 22.7 per cent of agricultural workers and those between fifteen and seventeen make up 23.3 per cent. Additionally, 44.6 per cent of children between six and fourteen work in fields, whereas this rate jumps to 92.7 per cent in the age group of fifteen to seventeen. This astonishingly high rate of child workers builds up Syrian families' precarity but also facilitates their survival in the highly competitive labour market. The precarization of Syrian labour largely depends on child labour in agricultural production.

The perception of children's labour: 'Children have no age!'

Child labour in seasonal agricultural work has deep roots in family-based labour in which children have been a significant component of not only agricultural work but also the generational skill transfer system. As a form of the contemporary labour regime in agriculture, seasonal work is more scrutinized in terms of children's involvement. In my fieldwork, I found no consistent view across employers, workers and labour intermediaries about child labour since different actors responded differently to the questions of who children are and what the law stipulates as the minimum age for agricultural work. The most distinct perspective emerging from my interviews is that the definition of childhood has little to do with age and may have different meanings. A child can be an individual of various ages. For this reason, the question of whether an intermediary or farmer employs any child workers usually draws the response of 'No, we never employ children'. However, many children actually work in the fields; what is clear from my fieldwork is that when a child passes the age of eleven or twelve, they are no longer considered to be children but persons with the ability to work. Additionally, children between the ages of fourteen and fifteen are seen as prime agricultural workers. For the community, the perception of children was not based on age criteria but on physical development and appearance criteria. Assessing childhood according to appearance and capabilities was often expressed with the saying, 'children have no age'. When children are able to understand and carry out the given work, they are considered as grown-up, no longer children. With no connection established between childhood and age, work becomes an issue of capacity: an individual's suitability to work is defined by 'being capable', being 'grown up enough' or 'having a knack'.

In contrast, the state of childhood is defined as someone playing games and not being able to understand or not yet able to reason. Many families define children as those under ten. As a working mother of four children stated:

> Child is not the one who can work in the field. When they can we don't call them children any more. For us, child has no age. Child is the one who is playing with toys and has no understanding. When they start doing useful stuff around and keep themselves busy with work, they are no longer children. We don't call them children anymore.

Syrian agricultural worker households also believe that children over twelve, not the adult members of families, should work in fields. A father, for example, explained that he could not do fieldwork due to his age and poor health, but his children are of an ideal age:

> Look at me. How can I go out and work in the fields? I am 40 years old with heart disease and cannot bend my back to stub up the soil. Their mother is so busy to cook and clean for our large family, but from time to time, she goes out harvesting when it is the high season. . . . Look, it is their job to work in the field, it is their prime age to be workers.

Many Syrian refugees I interviewed were not concerned about the high number of children under eighteen working in fields and appreciated their contribution. By breaking the link between the concept of child and their age as a mere number, Syrian refugees try to get ahead of the competition among the precariat to tap into informal jobs.

Why do children become workers?

The prevalence of child labour in the agricultural sector, worsened with the influx of Syrians, is justified mostly with poverty and as a survival mechanism for many families. When asked why children become workers, the most common response is the struggle to make ends meet and poverty mostly generated as a result of migration. Child labour is passed on from one generation to another, and this cultural, behavioural pattern has underlying economic reasons among families. Since agricultural intermediaries share the socio-economic background of migrant worker families, their perspective and experience of child labour reveal this same cultural, behavioural pattern. In seasonal agricultural production, the chief survival strategy of Syrian households is to direct as many members as possible to income-generating activities. Children are quite useful in the process. Since the number of people living in Syrian households is high, more people engaged in work bring in more income. The intersecting vulnerabilities embedded in child labour in Turkey's agricultural sector are illustrated in the following testimonies that show how Syrians justify their children's engagement under harsh working conditions. A father of six boys (forty-two years old) stated:

> I must accept that no child labour means no survival for us. I don't want to let them work but I have no other way. If they don't work, we have nothing to eat. Working is not shame, we work with our dignity. Instead of dying with

hunger, we go out there and work. I have six children. I cannot feed them on my own. That's why all my children work.

Other interviewees stated: 'We barely survive, I would not make them work if it was possible'; 'We do not go there for fun, they have to work so we will not go hungry'; 'We work with our dignity, so we will not have to depend on anyone else'; and 'Our family is crowded, we give up on school and employ children out of necessity'. All of these cases reflect families' reliance on child labour for survival.

Another distinctive feature of child work in agricultural production is relieving parents from work. Children's involvement in income generation may mean that parents and the elderly in the family can slowly withdraw from work life. When children start providing income for the family, at least the father usually stops working. When the two sons of a family living in a tent started working, for example, the parents withdrew from agricultural labour as the work was too difficult for people of a certain age. Child labour is justified with commonly held perceptions that only the young can do agricultural work, as adults are too 'old and ill' for such labour and that agricultural work is more suitable for children over the age of twelve or thirteen. Children are considered to be agile and healthy, while parents are worn out from years of arduous farm work. Parents are unable to continue working in fields due to various diseases and physical depletion. The prevalence of child labour is not just due to this perception but also a way to increase household income by having many household members, including children, work. For Syrian families engaged in agricultural work, children have significant income-earning potential.

For labour intermediaries, agricultural work is a method of both entertaining children (keeping them occupied with something) and helping to build a future for them, since most of these children drop out of school. One intermediary said, 'Should they wander around idly? At least they do something', illustrating that he sees child labour as a way to supervise children who, in most instances, could not continue their education and this was a means to protect them. Those who espouse opinions such as 'What will happen if they will not work' and 'they will either become thieves or go hungry' consider labour to have a disciplining effect on children. By getting work for their children and teaching them a profession, families strive to keep their children away from bad habits and environments. Children can acquire skills they would not be able to achieve in school. The field becomes their school, and work turns them into obedient and diligent workers.

Childcare and child labour are intricately intertwined. Some families bring their children to work since they have no place to leave them. While working in the field, families take care of their children and the children become accustomed to farm work. An agricultural intermediary expressed the situation as follows: 'We cannot leave them behind while we are working, so they are forced to be here with us and they work.' The desire to keep children under close watch and the absence of care services often lead to child labour.

Interviews revealed that agricultural intermediaries who find work for very young children think that they are helping poor families. Children's employment is generally rationalized through such excuses as 'They were very poor, I gave them work, they work for their bread.' Agricultural intermediaries who employ children act on the grounds that they are supporting the household budget and are helping the child to grow up as an experienced agricultural labourer. The result of these perceptions and attitudes is widespread child labour in agricultural production.

A child's work makes a day's wage!

Syrian families insistently bargain with their employers to bring their children to work. A labour intermediary explained the reason why children are the main agricultural workers and how Syrians ensure their children work in fields:

> The employers usually say, don't bring any children to his field. But what happens is that the worker families always bring along three or four children together. When we say to them that we do not want children, the families respond usually 'if you don't want them, we are not working either'. They count that if a child works, one earns a day's wage. So, they think that a child's work makes a day's wage.

Agricultural intermediaries stated that they do not want to hire children, but families certainly bring one or two children, sometimes more, with them to work. Intermediaries noted that they were unable to prevent child labour; if they refused to let children work, adults would not work either.

Along with the income children earn for their families, their labour is also seen as a way to control children, as discussed earlier. According to a farmer who is doing large-scale watermelon farming in his 100 acres of fields in Adana:

> We actually do not want children to come. But physically developed children are going to get into trouble if they do not come to work. Families want to have eyes on them all day.

The same employer also emphasized the fact that if children work in his watermelon fields he is not even aware of it as many decisions related to workers are left to *dayışbaşı* who is organizing his seasonal workers. Therefore, employers emphasized that they do not have much information about the composition of worker groups, since the agricultural intermediaries they work with are fully authorized to form labour pools. For this reason, from the perspective of employers, the responsibility of putting children at work lies with the families and agricultural intermediaries.

Every family member participates in the process however they can. Very young children do not necessarily work for pay, but they do engage in farm-related chores or work as unpaid labourers. Young children carry empty buckets, help fill or tie sacks, take care of smaller children and fetch and distribute water. Parents do not see child labour as providing daily wages alone; they also see it as a component of their own paid labour (Figure 5.7).

Children, especially young children, are not formally employed when work is paid by unit area and unit amount (or lump sum). For example, child labour is common in work on produce that is priced by unit amount or unit area (lump sum), such as the onion harvest. Everyone in the family works to collect a certain amount of produce or cover a certain amount of land. Cutting the stems of onions recently pulled from the soil is seen as children's work. Almost 30–35 per cent of the workers in the onion harvest are children, as young as five or six. Children working in this form of lump-sum system are therefore viewed as sources of free labour by both their families and employers. In fact, it only becomes possible for an adult worker to earn a full day's wage by using the labour of the children of the family. For instance, in a family harvesting onions, five children under the age of twelve, one young woman aged nineteen, and the mother and father can form a work team of eight. In this case, three adults earn full wages from onion work – which is tied to a daily output of eleven sacks of onions per individual – but this income is only possible with the contributions of the five children. Also, since the family makes a contract based on unit area

Figure 5.7 A boy picking cotton with his mother. Source: Development Workshop Archive.

or unit amount of produce, wages are determined in the form of a lump sum, and as long as the work is completed, neither the employer nor the agricultural intermediary is concerned about who the workers are or their age. What is essential is that the work is completed. Families work together from the early hours of the morning until late in the evening to maximize their income for the day. Although these types of roles are often brushed over by such statements as 'children are always carrying out light work', the truth is that children work intensely in the field.

The arrival of Syrian workers has affected the status of child labour in agricultural production. An increase in the labour supply as well as a reduction in labour costs in the Adana Plain has made it possible to allocate more labour and use more land in agricultural production. Agricultural intermediaries frequently noted that the arrival of Syrians increased child labour because child labour is more common among these migrant groups and there is no distinction between children and adults when daily wages are paid per individual. Syrian families are directing more children towards work in order to survive after migration and to meet their needs. The field/orchard owners and agricultural intermediaries go along with this practice during periods in which the demand for labour is very high.

Working conditions of children

Children's working conditions are expressed by their parents working for different products. For example, Berivan is from a cotton-picking family. The story of Berivan, a nine-year-old cotton-picking girl, illustrates the working conditions of children, women and all workers in a cotton field. Berivan is from a poor neighbourhood of the Eyyübiye district of Şanlıurfa. As a nine-year-old, she should be in the fourth grade. Because she was enrolled in school at an older age, she is currently in the second grade. Berivan started picking cotton alongside her family in mid-September. She will continue until the end of November. Her family consists of her, her two older brothers and her mother. On average, they can pick 350 kilograms of cotton daily. They, as the whole family, make TRY 150 per day. If they work for forty to fifty days, they will earn TRY 6,000–7,000 during the season. They have to get by with this money the whole winter. Berivan says that they wake up at 4.00 am every day, and after eating breakfast and packing their lunches, they arrive at the field at 6.00 am. They live in a tent near the cotton field. Even if the field is close to Şanlıurfa city centre, they prefer to live in the tent because they can save some time and there is no one to drive them back and forth. Berivan picks cotton all day until the evening. She can pick between 50 and 60 kilograms daily, which means a TRY 25–30 contribution to the family budget. She complains from the heat and from the back pain she suffers at night due to bending over all day long. She says there is no shade in the field to hide from the sun; during the lunch break all the workers gather together in the shade of the tractor. She says cotton harvest work is hard and she has to start school well after the semester has already started because she works. This affects her grades in school, she says.

A father who is a cotton sharecropper explains how his children are engaged in cotton production and how the division of labour for children is undertaken throughout the process:

> I take care of weeding, hoeing and harvesting in this cotton field with the help of my wife and our children. I manage other tasks, like irrigation, spraying and fertilizing on my own. If the children do not work alongside us, it will be impossible to earn any income from this job. Of course, the children's education is affected negatively. The harvest continues till early November. The children will be able to go to school only after that.

We have been working here since 1997. The job starts in May and ends in November. Anyone who is able to hold a hoe works. The children start at the age of 10, doing tasks they are able to do.

We live on the border of the field. We start working as soon as the sun rises. We work till the sun sets. We decide when we take a break, eat breakfast and lunch. It is as if we own the business. A 12-13-year-old child can pick 100 kilograms of cotton per day. That means TRY 35 earned per day. Children get tired a lot. When the harvest starts we work 12 hours every day, the harvest takes on average 45 days. All of us have lower-back pain. We pick cotton while bending over all day long. Sometimes the children's psychology deteriorates as well.

In addition to children's activities in cotton production, children actively work in greenhouses in the province of Mersin. Work in greenhouses is family work. Children are usually involved as unpaid family workers alongside women. Harsh working conditions and environmental factors make greenhouse work dangerous for children. In greenhouses, long working days, lifting and carrying heavy loads, working under extreme hot or cold weather and frequent traffic accidents during transportation of workers make these jobs dangerous for workers below the age of eighteen. Besides these factors, the chemicals and pesticides that are used extensively in greenhouse production pose serious risks to the health of child workers. Since safety precautions for dangerous tasks are in general not considered even for adult workers, these working environments may seriously damage the health of both child workers and the children in worker families even if they do not actively participate in the production process. These negative consequences can be long-lasting and may lead to serious complications in the future due to the accumulation of chemicals.

Education and work: That cannot go along well!

Syrian child workers in rural areas have had no chance to attend school in Turkey. During my five-year research with agricultural workers, I have not come across a single Syrian child attending school. This is a well-known and repeated adverse effect of seasonal agricultural work on children's education in general. The education of young children and high drop rates have been an important concern for Turkish agricultural worker families. They consider seasonal agricultural work to be a hindrance for children's educational attainment that feeds into a generational poverty trap.

Dropping out of school is a common practice among children engaged in seasonal agricultural work since they travel and live away from their usual residence for more than six months per year. Gender inequality within school dropouts is also observed during the field study: families place less importance on the education of girls than boys and a significant proportion of girls never attend high school. The cycle of low education attainment persists from generation to generation: parents typically reached low education levels and now their children cannot continue their education while they move with their families to work in agriculture. These children themselves become seasonal agricultural workers. Once the reasons for their children dropping out of school and working in the field are interrogated, agricultural workers present it as part of their misfortune: that children are also living their parents' fate. This fatalistic perception is expressed in such statements as 'they work because they have nothing else to do' and 'children of a poor person are poor, they become workers since they have no other alternative'. Education is one of the most important means of breaking the poverty cycle both for worker families and children; hence, we see the hindering impact of parental occupation and class status on possibilities of vertical, intergenerational and intragenerational mobility.

This situation is best illustrated with a case I encountered during one of my field research trips. A young labour intermediary explained to me how he took over the position from his brother when his brother was tired and quit his job as a labour intermediary. During the conversation, his brother entered the tent and joined in. We discussed such subjects as the decrease in wages and work opportunities and Syrians, typical topics of discussion with each of my interviews with agricultural worker families. Then, suddenly, the brother's young son came in. 'Look', said his father, 'I forced him over and over, he dropped out of school, and I went and enrolled him again and again. But still I couldn't keep him in school.' When we asked the young boy why he did not want to go to school, he replied: 'While my father was working to provide for seven people in our family, I was ashamed of attending school.' For some children, the affirmation of a sense of adulthood comes through working in fields and adding to the family budget; this may well feel more attractive than attending school.

The young boy's response was a kind of cold shower for us. Children attending school perceived themselves as useless consumers with no contribution. It is possible that children's perception is common in an environment where there are no role models who have had access to professional occupations after a successful academic life. Against positive images of working children who are productive and contribute to their families are negative images of schoolchildren who only consume. When I asked about the reasons why children were unable to continue their education, economic reasons and difficulties were provided as the leading cause. 'Children working in agriculture have low school success' was a commonly accepted reason by communities engaged in seasonal work. Families accept that agricultural work and education cannot go hand in hand and families painfully opt for fields rather than classrooms.

Work is also conceptualized as disciplining children who already dropped out of school. Propositions such as '[the child] did not finish school', '[the child] has no profession', 'better [for the child] to work rather than become a lowlife', '[the child] works as [the child] was unsuccessful in school', '[the children] work because they want to' and 'they have stopped going to school' illustrate that children are seen as responsible agents who can be disciplined and punished with work.

Accessing or continuing education is a significant problem for children working in agricultural production. Agricultural work causes children to miss the opportunity of a better future and prevents their social and cultural development. The low education level of families hinders the social and cultural growth of children as well. Since working families need to move once they are summoned for work, children either start school late or stop attending early and cannot complete a normal education cycle. As long as education remains inaccessible, this spiral of poverty will continue for generations.

A day of workers: From dawn to sunset

Morning for seasonal agricultural workers between 3.00 am and 4.00 am, the quietest time of the day elsewhere, is a time of extraordinary activity in the Doğankent neighbourhood of Adana. It is possible to see people hurrying around and to hear engine noises and anxious honking of cars. It is the start of another working day for the residents of Doğankent. Among those starting every day in such a hurry is Ahmet from Çermik, Diyarbakır, aged sixteen. So is his friend with whom he goes to work. They both smoke and neither has completed his compulsory eight years of basic education and they don't intend to. They have come to Doğankent with their families for seasonal agricultural work. They wake up at 4.00 am. Before heading to work, they queue up in front of a bakery for bread and buns and then wait for the old van to pick them up in the dark. Poverty has forced them and their families into the citrus fruit harvest. The combination of buns and tea in a plastic cup is breakfast for Ahmet and his friend. They rely solely on these buns for energy throughout the warm and difficult working day. In the short conversation I had with Ahmet and his friend, Ahmet told me that he would not attend high school, and that although his mother wanted him to enrol in the distance learning high school programme, he would not do so. I asked him about Syrian workers. He told me that they work for less than him and his friend, that their number had risen very quickly and that if things go on like this they would soon be out of a job (Figure 5.8).

Doğankent used to be a village in the Yüreğir district of Adana, of which it is now officially a neighbourhood under the new law on metropolitan municipalities. According to what I was told by inhabitants, it is a settlement

Figure 5.8 A group of workers in a field. Development Workshop Archive.

of 40,000, including the surrounding area. In the neighbourhood, 25 per cent of the population are now Syrian refugees and that their number is increasing every day. The plain offers work twelve months a year. In this neighbourhood, all available space, even stables, have been rented out to Syrians. Syrians pay TRY 5,000 a year to rent the stables. In the early hours of the morning, domestic and Syrian workers alike await the transport that will take them to the citrus orchards and pepper fields. Around 5.00 am, between thirty and forty of them squeeze into vans designed for fifteen to twenty people and head out without having had a proper breakfast. There are so many Syrian workers that only the darkness of the night obscures their number. Hundreds of vans take workers from Syria and Turkey to the fields. Between 5.00 am and 6.00 am, dozens of vanloads of workers emerge from every street to the main road. By the time the sun rises, the vans headed towards the fields are followed by the trucks into which they will pile the fruit that they harvest. The place is extraordinarily active and noisy. Yet, at 6.00 am there is no sign of the mad rush: Doğankent appears to be an ordinary and quiet neighbourhood. All the workers have either made it to their fields or are about to. They will work until the trucks are full of oranges and mandarins and then they will come back home. The next day the same hurried cycle will continue, as it does almost every day of the year. At the same time as the agricultural workers make it to their fields, factory workers, civil servants and office employees in other places are sound asleep. Yet the struggle for the survival of the poorest has already begun. We don't know if they go to bed early, but they definitely rise early.

Conclusion

Women and child labour are an indispensable part of seasonal agricultural work. Women and children not only provide cheap labour but also generate leverage for Syrian families to better compete for seasonal agricultural jobs. This chapter examined how Syrian women and child labour are used in the paid and unpaid activities that are directly related to production of low-cost crops that compete in international markets or support low wages of domestic consumers. This provided an analysis of intersecting vulnerabilities of women and child labour whose labour has been a part of the successful negotiation process of Syrians.

Women's work in the realms of production and social reproduction and women's unpaid labour are directly linked to the production of low-cost agricultural products. Women's labour is at the centre not only of survival strategies of Syrian families but also of sustainability of agricultural production since their labour is essential for social reproduction of farm labourers. Inclusion of women and children in agricultural labour markets has been analysed as the result of the fact that their labour is easily controlled by patriarchal and capitalistic relations. Co-operation between patriarchal relations and capitalist exploitation had led to the intensification of women's gendered subordination as well as the emergence of new forms of subordination.

The second part of the chapter has shown how the income-generating power of child labour has boosted the use of child labour in Turkey's agricultural sector as children between the ages of fourteen and seventeen are perceived to be the prime farmworkers whose physical strength and posture is viewed as ideally suitable. Syrian child workers have fewer opportunities in education and alternatives available to them to break away from hard labour in agriculture but are in destitute situations to submit to hard-working conditions as the new precariat of Turkey.

6

Bonded labour

Recruitment, remuneration and retention

Seasonal agricultural work in Turkey rests upon a specific work regime in which the agricultural labour market constantly tries to include the most vulnerable labour forms. The sector uses the powerful labour management practices of recruitment, remuneration and retention (3Rs) to bond labour to seasonal farm work. The 3Rs also fuel Turkey's agricultural sector's integration with the world economy and lower the cost of food production for the country's population. Further, this work regime allows access to cheap labour without a long-term build-up of labour institutions that would lead to better working conditions and labour solidarities. This labour regime depends largely on the role of labour intermediaries in recruiting, retaining and paying workers.

This system has led to multi-generation bonded labour in Turkey's seasonal agriculture. Bonded labour in Turkey's seasonal farm work is a context-specific organic way to expropriate surplus. The seasonal agricultural work regime bonds workers to a specific location and to specific work, not only through linking productive and reproductive labour but also through limiting the physical movement of labour by confining workers to certain places and jobs. To explore how the 3R labour regime works in Turkey's seasonal agricultural labour markets, this chapter analyses the 3Rs and the ways this system affects workers and exploits labour.

Recruitment: Labour intermediation

The history of labour intermediation services worldwide goes back to the nineteenth century. 'In agriculture it was a source of "gangs" of seasonal labour at harvest time. In garments it goes back to the early "sweating" system used in factories and workshops' (Barrientos, 2011:4). Intermediation services were usually associated with slavery, forced and unfree labour and the rise of the labour movement. With a move towards formal regulations governing labour markets in the twentieth century, the system was significantly transformed. The abolition of slavery and the implementation of labour legislation against associated forms of bonded labour in many countries were meant to have ended such practices. The advancement of free-market production and trade were postulated to involve the 'free' supply of labour by workers (Koettl, 2009). However, with the rise of globalization, intermediation services have re-emerged and proliferated, indicating that they had never completely disappeared and that their connection with forced and slave labour continues.

There is no commonly agreed-upon definition of labour contracting. It is associated with what the ILO terms a 'triangular employment relationship', where the legal employer is separate from the person for whom work is carried out. However, it is important to distinguish between formally registered companies that provide temporary staffing services and more informal or quasi-registered labour contractors (Barrientos, 2011: 5). While the number of registered employment firms has increased globally, the proliferation of these services is seen as contributing to increasing flexibility and liberalization of labour markets. Informal, or undocumented, labour intermediation services are more difficult to define and can take on many forms. Some informal services only supply labour, while other services look for a more qualified workforce and supply certain materials. Although the role of labour contractors varies from country to country and region to region, as Barrientos (2011: 5) notes, they undertake four main roles:

- Labour intermediary or contractor supplies workers to a producer for a fee, and the producer becomes the direct employer.
- Labour intermediary or contractor supplies workers to a producer. The agent pays the workers (taking a percentage), but the producer supervises the workers.
- Labour intermediary or contractor supplies workers to a producer on the basis of a contract for specific task, for which payment is made (e.g. clearing a field or embellishing a batch of garments); the agent or contractor pays the workers and supervises their work.

- Informal contractor – an individual (often a worker) who recruits other workers for a farm or factory, may also be a worker or ex-worker, and receives a payment or unofficially takes a deduction from wages.

The recent revitalization of labour intermediation services has been linked to the rise in flexible, temporal and seasonal work in the agriculture and manufacturing sectors. Labour intermediaries play a central role in the functioning and organization of seasonal work. For example, landowners do not advertise in newspapers for job openings or register with the state employment agency to find workers, nor do they send agents to schools and universities. When they need workers, farmers usually contact labour contractors and inform them how many workers they need. Agricultural intermediaries, on the other hand, recruit workers through their own relatives and present workers. Recruitment centred on social networks has many advantages for both labour contractors and farmers; labour intermediaries select those capable of undertaking the job from within their social circle and take on the responsibility of transferring skills to new recruits, and farmers can be reassured that workers have been screened.

The rise in demand for paid labour in agricultural production in recent years has led to the emergence of agricultural intermediaries who have established more professional relationships with their workers. According to Çetinkaya's study conducted in Adana, the professional or modern system of intermediation does not use blood relations (Çetinkaya, 2008). Over time, the study illustrates, those who used to work as seasonal migrant workers settled in Adana and are now seeking work through anonymous relationships. In spite of these trends, my research shows that many intermediaries continue to enter the labour force through relatives or via communal networks.

The absence of intermediation services would alter the landscape of agricultural production. Many workers would be unemployed and would spend more time searching for work, rather than be gainfully employed and earning needed wages for their families. Informal intermediation services make it possible for employers to have access to cheap sources of labour; absence of such services would undoubtedly drive up the costs of agricultural production. Furthermore, competition among intermediaries in their efforts to bid for jobs may too drive wages downwards (Vaupel and Martin, 1986).

Labour contractors recruit and supply local, internal and/or international migrant labour, depending on labour market conditions. Case studies indicate that recruitment of migrant labour in particular is increasing across the globe. Labour contractors, for example, have moved Asian workers to garment factories in Jordan, Egypt, Mauritius and Romania (Crisan, 2007; BSR, 2008; Maher, 2009). These migrant workers are often very vulnerable to abuse, as this recruitment often involves high levels of exploitation and sometimes new forms of forced labour. In a study of 600 returned foreign contract labourers in four countries (Indonesia, Philippines, Thailand and Vietnam), Verité (2005) found systematic abuse, including placement fees, high charges (such as for travel), onerous debt burdens and 'runaway insurance' (against a worker absconding). Undocumented migrants are often most vulnerable to conditions of unfree labour, especially when locked into a dependent relationship with particular labour intermediaries through a system of effective debt bondage (Verité, 2005; Pollard, 2006). Labour contractors often charge migrant workers high fees for transport, training and provision of 'documents', and also charge high 'interest' on loans for these 'services'. These charges are often on top of high payments to agents for 'travel' to the country of destination. Undocumented migrant workers often have no channels for claiming their rights and fear not only loss of work but also deportation if they complain.

The following section focuses on the system of Turkish labour intermediation services and the role of labour intermediaries in regulating the labour markets of seasonal agricultural work. I derive the findings in this section from research conducted in the provinces of Adana and Şanlıurfa with labour intermediaries. This research, applied through a questioner including structured questions, collected information from 141 labour intermediaries and 24 in-depth interviews in April 2017.

Turkish intermediaries recruiting Syrian refugees: Who are labour intermediaries?

In Turkey, labour intermediaries organize almost all of the seasonal agricultural workforce. As workers and their families move from one province to another to undertake different tasks in agricultural production, they either move with an intermediary or contact one when they reach a site of production. Contractors in Turkey are referred to by such names as '*amele başı*', '*elçi*', '*dayıbaşı*' and '*simsar*', most widely interchangeably used ones are *dayıbaşı* and *elçi*. Based on my research, labour contracting is a male-dominated occupation (with 95.7 per cent male). They are from an overwhelmingly farmworker background. While their average age is forty-four, almost 30 per cent are between forty and forty-nine. Because of the common practice of starting work as young as age ten or twelve, workers reach maturity when they are quite young and some become an intermediary. So, they become intermediaries after many years of working in agricultural production themselves and when they reach their mid-thirties, they typically start working as intermediaries. When they reach their thirties, workers may have already accumulated twenty to twenty-five years of work experience. Since most intermediaries were child workers themselves, they have a more tolerant attitude towards child labour.

Labour intermediaries live in relatively large households. The average rural household comprises nine people.[1] Access to a large labour pool and a wide circle of relatives constitutes a strategic advantage. Intermediaries can initially rely on their own immediate family members and distant relatives to form their worker teams. Intermediaries tend to have lower educational attainment than the general population. Based on my research, the largest group consists of graduates of five-year primary schools with 32.6 per cent, primary school dropouts follow with 17.7 per cent and illiterates with 12.8 per cent. Being a part of agricultural production hinders access to education and this hindrance persists in their life cycle and throughout the generations. Labour intermediaries are not exceptions to the structural and systemic problems of poverty, unavailability of public services and lack of alternative opportunities.

In recent years, the main source of agricultural workers comes from a south-eastern province of Turkey, Şanlıurfa, where the majority of labour intermediaries (64 per cent) were born. Şanlıurfa not only is traditionally a source of agricultural labour but in recent years also has hosted a large number of Syrian refugees. This is the main reason for focusing on labour intermediaries, which is ideal for the study and precarization of Syrian workers.

Registration and informality

Turkish Law 4904 on the Turkish Employment Agency regulates intermediation services in agriculture. Anyone who wants to be a labour intermediary in theory must apply to Turkey's Employment Agency (İş-Kur) to obtain the Certificate on Employment Intermediation in Agriculture. The certificate is available for a fee (annually determined), valid for three years, which has to be stamped every year to be valid and has to be renewed at the end of three years. For every intermediary, an Intermediary Record, the content of which is determined by the authorities, is kept by the relevant provincial or branch directorates.[2] Almost anyone who applies to İş-Kur can get a certificate and be a labour contractor. But even though the certification process is easy, the vast majority of contractors bypass it. As agricultural work itself, labour intermediation is mostly informal work.

The extent of informality is most visible when comparing actual registration numbers with the estimated number of contractors. The provinces of Adana and Şanlıurfa host the highest number; in 2017, 345 intermediaries were registered in these two provinces. Meanwhile, the Çukurova Agricultural Intermediaries Association expressed that there were approximately 2,000 agricultural intermediaries living in the villages/neighbourhoods of Adana alone. For the Şanlıurfa province the number is estimated to be between 500 and 600 people (Development Workshop, 2018). However, even these estimates are low since many more work in secluded rural settings. The data I collected reveal that of the 141 labour intermediaries only 46 per cent held a certificate. Among those who did not have a certificate, 81.6 per cent stated that that they did not obtain the certificate 'because no one asked for it'. This is expected in a system where work is carried out informally and where control, inspection and sanction systems relating to the rules on working as agricultural intermediaries and obtaining intermediation certificates are not effective.

The informal nature of their work is also evident in their disregard for other legal 'requirements' in the agricultural sector. Seasonal migrant agricultural workers have to undertake long journeys between provinces to arrive in locations where they want to work. While the vehicles used for the transportation are required to have proper and necessary documents along with vehicle inspection reports showing that they meet certain standards, agricultural intermediaries who transport dozens of workers from one city to another have little concern for this documentation and standards. When agricultural workers arrive at their destination and stay in temporary settlements or dwellings of field/orchard owners or places they rent, their credentials are recorded by the closest gendarmerie or police station.

Agricultural intermediaries organize such procedures, and for that reason they are constantly in communication with security forces. Even though many of them have no certificate, they continue to operate informally. Such cases confirm that none of the sanctions and inspections specified in regulations are enforced even by criminal officers.

Regulatory roles: Dependency and exploitation

Labour intermediaries provide a variety of services to agricultural workers. Organization of transportation from workers' usual residential province to and from their workplace is one of the main duties of intermediaries. Since the camps or tent settlements are many kilometres away from city centres, intermediaries usually provide transportation to workers when they arrive at the camp areas. Except in emergency cases, such as childbirth or injury, workers have access to health-care services only with the help of their agricultural intermediary. In some cases, intermediaries help workers overcome language barriers and cultural differences which might arise between employers and workers (Kusadokoro et al., 2016). Labour intermediaries' Arabic-language skills also help to facilitate the process of attracting Syrian labour. Kurdish and Arab labour intermediaries solve workers' language problems. On the one hand, they are among the few people who can communicate with Syrian refugees, thus making the latter's life much easier in Turkey. This also results in the Syrians' dependency on labour intermediaries. An intermediary illuminated his indispensable role due to his language ability:

> I am working here as a labour intermediary. I speak Arabic. The landowners don't speak Arabic. Actually, there is nobody here who speaks Arabic. If I am not here, Syrians cannot work because the landowners and workers couldn't understand each other. Arabic is quite handy for me at this time because I can recruit Syrians and come here to work.

Since worker households residing in tent settlements do not have direct access to shops, it is through intermediaries they can acquire even basic consumer goods, such as fruits, vegetables, legumes and detergents. By making agreements with traders or salespersons, intermediaries arrange the arrivals of trucks or minibuses to the settlements at regular intervals and the purchase of consumer goods by workers. Since workers do not receive their payment immediately upon completion of work, purchases might be made using advances given to them by the intermediary or on credit. Intermediaries have an influence, albeit indirect, on how workers spend the money they earn from their labour (Support to Life, 2014).

Studies investigating the role of agricultural intermediaries frequently underline the dominating and exploitative aspects of the relationship between intermediaries and workers. The commissions (so-called service fees) that intermediaries deduct from the wages paid to the workers exemplify such domination and exploitation. Commissions can be as high as 10 per cent of the workers' wages. A study on seasonal agricultural workers in the Adana province showed that in 2016, workers' daily rates were between TRY 44 and 45, and between TRY 4 and 5 of this rate was paid to intermediaries as commission (Semerci and Erdoğan, 2017). In addition, workers' wages were not paid in cash but in the form of cards on which the name of the agricultural intermediary is placed. Workers were given one card for each day of work (Semerci and Erdoğan, 2017). They, however, do not receive their payment at the end of the period of work but at certain times of the year.

The dependency relationship between intermediaries and workers derives from the fact that intermediaries come from large families and close-knit communities and most of the workers are their relatives, neighbours or acquaintances from the same part of the country. Placing informal and personal relations at the centre of agricultural production, this relationship strengthens trust and solidarity between workers and intermediaries. Intermediaries expect loyalty from workers; workers are to be dependent on them rather than on their employers, unlike in formal employment relations. Employment as a result of social networking facilitates solidarity, dependency and mutual trust to be the defining aspects of work relations rather than the formal principles of labour relations.

Workers incur debt to intermediaries during periods when there is no work or when they need cash, showing another aspect of this dependency and exploitation. Intermediaries offer workers cash advances in winter or even during the work season when workers need cash (since they do not receive payment immediately). Workers rely on these advances for their livelihood, necessities or emergencies. Consequently, intermediaries guarantee that workers will work for them during the peak agricultural season. This dependency affects the entire work relationship. Any objection raised by workers to the amount of payment, their working hours or work conditions is regarded as 'ingratitude and disloyalty' (GNAT, 2015). Since labour intermediaries help their workers financially year-round they expect to have total royalty and acceptance of worst working conditions.

Forming worker teams and recruiting refugee labour

Another distinctive feature of recruitment in agricultural production is the necessity to form teams of ten to fifteen workers. Each team is supervised by an intermediary who, in addition to recruitment, trains, organizes and dismisses workers, as needed. Intermediation services allow employers to find sufficient numbers of workers at the right time to fulfil specific production needs without much personal effort and financial resources spent on recruitment.

Forming worker teams is a manifestation of power intermediaries have over workers and their families. Semerci and Erdoğan (2017) emphasized intermediaries' authority:

> The agricultural intermediary decides who gets to work where, in which field and on which task; and gives privileged treatment to his own relatives and people close to him. (Semerci and Erdoğan, 2017: 30)

Some of the questions intermediaries have to tackle include: Who will comprise the teams? Which members of a given family will be part of the team? To what extent will adults, women and children be included? They base their decisions on the nature of work, employers' demands, wage levels and workers' qualifications. In forming worker teams, intermediaries rely on their resources, derived from their experience and social capital.

Having an agricultural labour background (experience and leadership) and, perhaps more importantly, coming from a large family and being able to engage fellow townsmen (social relations) constitute the pillars of the social capital required to become an agricultural intermediary in Turkey. Intermediaries' capacity in accessing and mobilizing the labour force in agricultural production is determined by these factors. Data from my fieldwork show (Table 6.1) that 26.4 per cent of workers are family members and relatives, 18.9 per cent are friends and close associates, 9.5 per cent are people from the same neighbourhood and 8.4 per cent are close relatives of current workers. Interestingly, the remaining 36.8 per cent are Syrian workers. This

Table 6.1 Sources of Labour for Recruitment in Adana

Labour sources	Number	%
Potential workers recommended by workers in the teams	8	8.4
Relatives	25	26.4
Friends and/or acquaintances	18	18.9
People living in the neighbourhood of intermediaries	9	9.5
Syrian migrants	35	36.8
Total	95	100.0

result indicates a change in the composition of worker groups mobilized since one-third of the workers are Syrian, pointing to a possible shift in recruitment strategies.

On average, an intermediary controls seventy-six workers. Worker teams are made up of 37.5 per cent adult women, 34.7 per cent adult men. While 10.7 per cent are girls and 10.4 are boys between the ages of fifteen and seventeen, 3.4 per cent are girls and 3.4 per cent are boys under age fourteen. The results indicate that 27.9 per cent of the labour composition is composed of individuals under the age of eighteen, which confirms earlier findings on seasonal agricultural workers reporting the rate of child labour to be one-third of the total workforce. While the minimum age for seasonal migrant agricultural labour, which is one of the worst forms of child labour, is eighteen years, my Adana study shows that about 30 per cent of the workers contracted by agricultural intermediaries are under the age of eighteen, with girls and boys employed about equally. Another aspect of the labour force composition is women workers. Overall women and young girls make up 51.6 per cent of the total labour force. Approximately 37 per cent are adult women, while adult men comprise 34 per cent. It was often cited during fieldwork by many respondents that 'agriculture is women's business' and 'there is no agricultural production without women'.

The worker composition of labour intermediaries confirms the recent phenomenon of Syrian agricultural workers in Turkey. As the number of Syrians is increasing rapidly in agricultural jobs, a significant number of domestic seasonal workers are withdrawing from agricultural production. A 2016 Development Workshop report shows that agricultural production in Adana is gradually being handed over to Syrian migrant workers; hence, the tent settlements of agricultural workers have been occupied by Syrian migrant families (Development Workshop, 2016). The ratio of Syrian migrants in the worker teams of agricultural intermediaries who participated in my research in Adana confirms the findings of the Development Workshop report. A total of 71.6 per cent of the agricultural intermediaries said that they have been working with Syrian workers.

Frequent statements expressing that the number of workers from Turkey are dropping due to the influx of Syrian migrant workers indicate that these figures may be even higher. In many interviews, intermediaries reported that for some time workers from Şanlıurfa, referred to as 'local workers', no longer come to Adana and are now replaced by Syrians. In fact, the presence of foreign migrant labour has advantages for both agricultural production and agricultural intermediaries in the Adana Plain. Syrian participation in agricultural production has enabled field/orchard owners to reduce production costs by dropping wages or by avoiding an increase in wages paid to nationals. Agricultural intermediaries, on the other hand, benefit from this situation in some cases by employing Syrian workers at very low wages and keeping their commissions higher. This situation has resulted in the rapid spread of Syrian migrant workers throughout the Adana Plain and definitely has had a worsening impact on the problem of child labour. Newly arrived migrants usually have as many members of the family as possible employed.

This shift in the labour force has led to Syrian workers reaching out to intermediaries, sometimes in person and sometimes upon recommendation, rather than through acquaintances. Almost half of the agricultural intermediaries stated that Syrian migrants came to them by recommendation, while 30.9 per cent said that Syrian migrants contacted them directly. Only 14.7 per cent of intermediaries reach out to Syrian migrants but they are the ones who are living in the same village, neighbourhood or tent area. Only 8.8 per cent of the intermediaries contact Syrian migrant workers through their relatives (Table 6.2).

With the onset of Syrian workers' participation in agricultural production in Adana, personal social relations in mobilizing labour are less critical. Different criteria than family bonds and personal relations have gained importance. Reputation and credibility of the intermediary and the trustworthiness of workers insured with recommendations have become more important in this more anonymous relationship. As most of the

Table 6.2 Methods for Worker Recruitment

Recruitment methods	Number	%
I contact workers upon recommendation	31	45.6
My relatives	6	8.8
Live in the same village, neighbourhood, tent group	10	14.7
They contact me to ask for work	21	30.9
Total	68	100.0

intermediaries are from Turkey and have no kinship with Syrian migrant workers, evaluating intermediaries' reliability and workers' trust becomes crucial. The unfortunate events that took place in the first years of Syrians' arrival, when many individuals acting as agricultural intermediaries placed Syrian migrant workers into work and disappeared without paying their wages, show how important the credibility of the agricultural intermediary is for agricultural workers.

Remuneration: Payment of workers

In agricultural production, various systems of payment are used. How wages are calculated and how they are paid to workers are distinctive features of agricultural labour markets. In Turkey's seasonal agricultural labour markets, labour intermediaries are central in transmitting cash earnings to workers and hold power over the method and timing of payments. Transmission of payments is often used to bond agricultural workers to a certain intermediary and to a certain period of time. Advance payments made to worker families guarantee their bondage and sustain their work. The following discussion is an evaluation of the payment system and the ways it works to bond seasonal agricultural labour in Turkey.

Major wage systems in seasonal agricultural work

In agricultural labour markets, several major wage systems are used, including hourly, daily, piece rate or incentive pay, and monthly salaries. Martin (2016) distinguishes the hourly and piece-rate wage systems by historical and labour force composition. For example, he mentions that most jobs in industrial countries pay hourly wages. The introduction of minimum hourly wages for farmworkers in most industrial countries and the increased homogeneity of the labour force, mostly young migrant men picking fruit in trees and mostly women picking berries and flowers, have encouraged more farm employers to pay hourly wages. On the other hand, he emphasizes that piece rate or incentive pay used to be more common in the past when the farm workforce was more diverse, including children and older workers. Under the piece-rate system, farm employers could hire everyone who wanted to work and not worry about the variance in productivity between workers, since the farm employer paid only for the work accomplished. While Martin's examination is based on industrial country experiences and international farmworkers, his analysis is applicable to the main wage systems used in seasonal agricultural labour markets.

In Turkey's agricultural sector, a variety of wage systems are used. The main types are daily wage, piece rate, monthly/seasonal salaries, sharecropping and unpaid work of women and children, which is an integral part of most wage systems. Different factors – such as crop type, performed activity, skill requirements and geography – affect which wage system is preferred. The nature of tasks performed and skill requirements can result in different wage rates for workers. For example, such tasks as pruning bushes and trees and irrigating fields require less labour but more skilled workers than picking cotton or hazelnuts. Workers undertaking such tasks mainly come from the local population and have the power to determine their own wages.

For harvesting work, the need is for less-skilled labour but a greater number of workers; therefore, wage rates are usually quite low. As the minimum wage is rarely applied in agriculture, local wage rates are determined jointly by the provincial wage commissions composed of local governmental representatives, farmers, labour intermediaries and traders. For example, in the Adana Plain, known for crop variety, widespread production and need for seasonal workers, wage rates in orange picking are determined by the consensus of the Çukurova Agricultural Intermediaries Association, the union of farmers, the chamber of agriculture and the associations of exporters, whereas in other areas, the *muhtars* (village heads) and farmers set wage rates. While commission members change from one place to other, one common underlying character of these commissions is that workers have no or little control over wage rates and wage commissions.

My fieldwork reveals four different wage systems: a daily wage, piece rate, sharecropping and salaries.[3] These different systems have an impact on how skill, age, gender and ethnic composition of workers and the worker teams are formed. For example, the daily wage system requires individual workers, whereas the piece rate is usually undertaken by families performing together as a unit. The remainder of this section focuses on the relationship of the four wage systems in agricultural work and labour formations.

A daily wage (*yevmiye*) is paid to workers after the completion of one day's work. It is generally used for preharvest tasks, such as hoeing, weeding, irrigating and spraying. *Yevmiye* is the dominant wage type for products that require a high degree of manual work and skill during harvesting (e.g. harvesting of hazelnuts, cherries, tea, strawberries, vegetables, olives and apples). In return for daily wages, workers are expected to work for a certain amount of time or produce a certain amount of output. For example, in the citrus fruit harvest, a team of workers is expected to harvest between one and two truckloads of lemons, oranges or grapefruits, depending on the height of the citrus trees; their wage does not depend on how many hours it takes to fill the quota. The daily work, typically, is not measured by the time spent at work but by the amount and quality of the output. As long as they produce the output, they receive the agreed-upon day wage

Another example of daily wage work is cherry picking. A cherry farmer in Eskişehir explains his work and labour needs by emphasizing that the cherry is a highly delicate product requiring extra care since most of the harvest is exported. The harvest is usually performed by climbing tall trees, sometimes with the help of a ladder. Cherry trees should not be harmed during picking. A regular workday starts at 6.00 am and lasts twelve hours, ending at 6.00 pm. Therefore, it is important for farmers to hire workers who have the physical strength and skill to complete the task. A cherry farmer explains his work in the following statement:

> Around 2,000-2,500 seasonal workers come to our district every year. They usually come from Şanlıurfa. In recent years, the number of Syrians among workers has increased. Most of those come to work in poppies, sugar beet, rice paddy, sunflowers hoeing and harvesting, and picking apples and cherries. They work from March until November. Most workers travel to this area through the arrangement of agricultural intermediaries. . . . We pay daily wages for apple and cherry harvest. The work starts at 6.00 am and

ends at 6.00 pm on most of the days. . . . The utmost attention is need[ed] in cherry picking since the product is delicate and trees can be easily harmed. . . . Farmers are under quite budgetary stress to survive and would like to get most with a minimum cost. We are always looking out to cut labour cost down so that we can survive in this competitive world. . . . We employ families working together. Men, women, girls and boys, everybody works. But we employ only children if they are older than 12 years of age. Children are more flexible and perform better on trees. At the end of the day, the physical appearance determines whether a child will be employed or not and it is usually the father's decision who goes to work in a family. So, the age written on the ID card does not matter in any ways.

Under piece-rate (*kabala*) wages, farm labour costs are fixed regardless of labour productivity, but worker earnings vary depending on how fast they work. Piece-rate wages are common when it is hard to regulate the pace of work, as when workers climb trees to pick fruit and are thus often out of sight of supervisors, and when quality is less important. The piece rate is used in Turkish agriculture to harvest a certain land size or amount of output. Such crops as cotton, onions and red peppers are priced by kilogram or sack. In onions, payments are received per sack for harvesting, cutting, cleaning and packaging. In the hoeing of sugar beets, poppy seeds, vegetable cultivation and weeding work, piece rate is calculated for a unit area. In cotton harvesting, piece rate is based on the weight of cotton collected. In piece-rate work, farmers are not concerned about who or how many people work but about how much is collected or harvested.

Piece-rate work means intense and hard work for agricultural labourers. A labour intermediary divides the work among different families who work as teams, and almost all family members – the elderly, women, including pregnant women, and children – are involved in the production. The goal is to carry out as much work as possible in a day to increase total income. Child labour is prevalent in the piece-rate wage system; even children as young as five or six can participate in some capacity. For example, during the onion harvest, they carry empty buckets, hold and tie sacks, load and distribute water to working family members and prepare meals.

In sharecropping (*yarıcılık/ortakçılık*) a landowner allows a tenant to use the land in return for a share of the crops produced on the land. Sharecropping has a long history; a wide range of situations and types of agreements have used this payment system. Since the cropper pays in shares of his harvest, owners and croppers share the risks of harvests being large or small and of prices being high or low. Because tenants benefit from larger harvests, they have an incentive to work harder and invest in better methods.

The Turkish term *yarıcılık* means taking half of the end product, while *ortakçılık* refers to any kind of sharecropping partnership, not necessarily involving a half-and-half sharing system. A special form of sharecropping, called 30 per cent, is practised in cotton production in Şanlıurfa where the cropper takes over every single task of cotton production (preparing the soil, planting the seeds, irrigating, spraying, weeding and picking) and gets paid 30 per cent of the end product in kind or cash. In some arrangements, the cropper undertakes all costs of input and labour while in others only the cropper provides the labour. How the crop is shared varies depending on the negotiations between sharers and croppers. Croppers are usually local landless farmers or poor urban dwellers who work in agricultural jobs during the high season. Here is the story of Mehmet, a cotton sharecropper in Şanlıurfa:

> The field owner is not able to supervise or run day-to-day operations. He has other business, other obligations. That is why I manage instead as a *kürekçi*,[4] I take care of everything as if it is my own property. It makes sense, since I am going to get 30 per cent of the harvested cotton in the end, in return for my services. Therefore, I should do the best I can. The better I perform, the more cotton will be harvested and so I will make more money as a result. I do not own any land myself. I do not want to leave my village to go to work elsewhere. If I stay here, I have to be a *kürekçi*. The landowner does not pay us our share from the government subsidies and support payments. I only receive 30 per cent from whatever price the cotton ginnery pays.

The salary wage system is more common in the activities of livestock care, horse breeding, greenhouse work and fig harvesting. However, monthly wages do not mean that the work continues for a twelve-month period; it is likewise seasonal and usually ends in nine or fewer months. In the fig harvest, a salary is paid only for the duration of the harvest. In greenhouse vegetable production, monthly wages are paid for a nine-month period. For shepherds, monthly or seasonal wages are paid for the duration of the grazing period. In some regions, in addition to seasonal wages, employers provide basic foodstuffs and a certain amount of harvested product. Monthly salary payments in agricultural production are quite rare and cover the workers, such as permanent farm staff, shepherds or greenhouse workers.

Most of Turkey's greenhouse production takes place in Antalya, Mersin, Adana and Muğla provinces. Mersin is the epicentre of Turkey's greenhouse production, with its 25 per cent share of the total production. Established by small-scale entrepreneurs with a certain amount of capital, greenhouses are mostly run by their initial investors; however, sometimes they have been rented or handed over to others. The products are marketed to the provinces located in the eastern Anatolia region and are not for export. The labour requirement is met through hiring a family on site. The worker family usually lodges in a hut near the greenhouses and only one salary is paid to the family, even though almost all family members are involved in the production.

One worker may be responsible for a 3-decare greenhouse. If the greenhouse in question is larger than 3 decares, the worker's wife and/or children may also participate in the production. During my summer 2017 fieldwork, the monthly salary paid was around TRY 1,000. During interviews with a group of greenhouse farmers, it is also stated that 'since Syrian workers are working at lower wages, the increase in the monthly wage levels in greenhouse production, which was TRY 600-700 6 or so 7 years ago, has stopped and then did not increase much'. It was also mentioned that 'in case when wives or children work alongside the worker, they are also paid separately with a monthly salary'. However, the salary is paid collectively to the family, not to an individual.

Landowners cover housing and utility expenses. Once per week, workers receive a certain amount of vegetables – such as tomatoes, peppers and eggplants – that are grown in the greenhouses. The landowner partially covers some living expenses of the worker families. The provision of boarding and food on top of a salary makes this wage system attractive to Syrian migrant families who want to save on rent and living expenses.

The wage cards as a payment method and the circulation of cash

In Turkey's seasonal agricultural labour markets, the specific wage payment practice helps to keep worker teams bonded to labour intermediaries and farm work. Salaries, piece rate and day wages are paid to labour intermediaries but not to individual workers. Then, labour intermediaries give wage cards to workers as a token of their working days. Compared to the wage payment systems in manufacturing and service sectors, wages earned in agriculture are first paid to the labour intermediary and then to a head of the family collectively, instead of to each worker individually. Since working as a family or a team is common practice in agriculture, sometimes wages are paid according to the collective performance of a family or a team of workers. In addition, wages are paid in rare instalments, not on a regular basis. This system ties workers to a particular intermediary and agricultural work.

In 2017, the daily wage for agricultural work in the Adana Plain was TRY 56 in gross; after TRY 6 was paid to intermediaries as commission, the daily net payment received by a worker decreased to TRY 50. Intermediaries occasionally pay families some advance in order to form their worker teams and keep their workers bonded to themselves before their yearly journey starts. They keep an account of the number of days and a family time sheet recording each day worked per worker in a specific family. After a day of work, a *wage card* is given to each individual worker (Figure 6.1).

Each wage card equals a day's wage and includes the intermediary's photo, name and telephone number. Even though no monetary amount is declared on these cards, a card is equal to a cash amount equal to one day's wage. The card states, 'No claim can be made if the card is lost.' Workers are paid in cash only at certain intervals. After receiving an upfront payment from a labour intermediary to cover their daily expenses and cost of travel, seasonal agricultural workers commonly receive a significant portion of their payment long after they complete the work. Workers usually get their wages from the intermediary after employers sell their product and receive their due payments. For example, workers employed in cauliflower sowing work in September get their wages months later, in January, after the farmer sells the crop and gets his payment. He then pays the intermediary, who finally pays the workers.

The delayed payment to workers is one of the ways both farmers and intermediaries retain the workforce by discouraging their leave from the team before their balance is cleared. If workers were paid daily, there would be a risk that they would not show up for work the following day. Postponing wage payments is one of the methods to ensure that the labour force will be working for the same agricultural intermediary in the field the next day. Also, payment in bulk at the end of a long period requires workers to maintain longer

Figure 6.1 A sample of a wage card. Source: Development Workshop Archive.

relationships with intermediaries. One of the families I interviewed stated that intermediaries pay their wages only in two instalments per year, in January and August. The control agricultural intermediaries hold over wages and the commissions they deduct from these wages ensures that the labour force they employ in their teams is kept in line and continues to work for at least a season. This relationship of control and dominance naturally affects working conditions and increases workers' tendency to work for the same agricultural intermediary for longer periods.

In some cases, workers are deceived by intermediaries, farmers or traders and never get paid for all or any of the days they worked. During my fieldwork, many workers reported that intermediaries disappeared without paying their workers, or farmers did not pay the wages at all. Agricultural workers stated that payments are often not made on time, leading to significant financial difficulties for families. The story of Uncle Hasan, a Syrian refugee in Adana, is a telling one and he expressed himself:

> Money is a piece of paper, but labour? Uncle Hasan's labour has become a piece of paper. At the tent site that sits right next to the shanty town in Adana, everyone except for the family of the agricultural intermediary are Syrians. We sat in the tent of Uncle Hasan and other families came to see what we were there for. We shared the tea made with little to spare. Uncle Hasan is grateful that Turkey is protecting them, that it has opened its borders for them. He says Turkey is the greatest nation on earth and may Allah protect it. It has not been long since he has settled in Adana and he says that they will spend the winter in the tent site and work as long as they can get jobs. His is a household with ten children and even putting food on the table takes a lot of income. He told us they had arrived in Adana recently, that they cannot find work and cannot get paid even if they find work. With a leap, Uncle Hasan goes up to the bridge and opens a pencil case that was on the fridge. It is full of pay slips with the names of agricultural intermediaries written on them. There are almost more than 100 cards of different colours. Each of them stands for a day of unpaid labour. They sit in the pencil case, as though to show that Uncle Hasan's and his families labour is nothing but a piece of paper. As it has no value, there is no reason to hide it or keep it under lock. The pieces of paper lie there, where anyone can see or take them. Pieces of paper which represent days of labour.

These pieces of paper, these wage cards, are worthless until they are redeemed with labour intermediaries.

Since cash flow is rare and is acquired twice or three times a year, wage cards act as a type of currency for workers. Because migrant seasonal agricultural workers usually stay in a location away from a city centre, supplies for basic needs are usually provided by labour intermediaries or mobile or stationary tradesmen contracted to sell foodstuff. Worker families can pay the price of their transactions to agricultural intermediaries or contracted shopkeepers with these cards. In my fieldwork, I came across an agricultural intermediary who set up a small shop in a neighbourhood heavily inhabited by agricultural workers in the Adana Plain selling basic consumption goods – pasta, flour, rice, crack wheat, sugar and tea and basic garments, such as sneakers and clothing – in exchange for wage cards. These cards are occasionally accepted as a sort of currency by wholesalers who work with intermediaries or 'mobile markets' that visit tent settlements.

In this wage-card currency system, intermediaries play a significant role. While the cards are used to lessen the economic difficulties experienced due to late payments of wages, they also generate a secondary source of income for intermediaries; through this system, intermediaries sell basic goods at higher prices than the standard market price. While workers, including women and children, are exploited by their employers, they are also exploited by intermediaries who seize their payment and control their labour and income throughout the process.

The payment made to the head of families is another way of retaining and controlling labour in seasonal agricultural work. Regardless of whether the head of a family works or not, labour intermediaries pay the male head of the household. In a tent area in Adana, where agricultural workers from Şanlıurfa were staying, a Syrian man between the ages of forty and forty-five reported that he was too sick and too old to work. Even though his two sons and daughter worked in the field, he tracked their payment. In another Syrian family, the man, introduced as the head of the family, did not work in the field but collected everyone's wages.

Retaining labour: Isolation and confinement in tent settlements

Retention strategies are employed to ensure that workers remain in their jobs for at least one season. In agricultural production, very few producers have formal human resources assessment and retention systems in place. Especially in greenhouse agriculture and shepherd work, a commonly used method of retention is to provide workers with accommodation year-round and to treat workers like members of the family. Employers who have to hire workers in teams delegate the task of communicating or establishing relations with workers to agricultural intermediaries rather than dealing with them directly or individually. Team-based hiring and retention are fundamental functions of the agricultural labour market (Martin, 2016).

In Turkey's seasonal agricultural labour markets, isolated locations and insufficient infrastructure of tent settlements are ways to keep the workforce confined and bonded and render workers' rejection of work close to impossible since they have no option to go back to their homes or independently travel to another location. This has reduced workers' 'bargaining power', suggested by Ben Rogaly (1996: 155), that determines working conditions and wages. The idea the 'poorer the workers' the 'better [the] job agreement' (Rogaly, 1996:155) can be translated into the idea that less mobile migrants make an even better precariat. The precarization of Syrian labour is affected not only by the living arrangements but also by the recruitment of the agricultural labour force, organization into working teams and transportation to the fields. Syrian workers are especially vulnerable because they have no safety nets and no option but to submit to the conditions offered to them in Turkey's seasonal agricultural labour market.

Tent settlements and shelter conditions

Living conditions of seasonal workers are often a great threat to the well-being of all workers. Worker families are typically accommodated in unsuitable tents offering little protection from the elements. In 2010, the Turkish government issued a Prime Ministerial Circular, the Improvement of Working and Living Conditions of Seasonal Migratory Agricultural (METİP), which has a goal of eliminating the problems that migrant seasonal agricultural workers face, including issues related to accommodations. The state introduced METIP camps as one solution to the problem of accommodations. METİP camps, very broadly, are made up of tents, and have power and running water, but with only two to three toilets for every one thousand residents, and limited bathroom facilities. METİP camps are generally for domestic migrant workers, although some Syrians have settled in these camps along with migrant seasonal agricultural worker families from Şanlıurfa, Mardin and Adıyaman.

The main motivation behind the creation of METİP camps is to prevent conflicts over ethnic identity and to keep poor Kurds out of sight and out of town centres (KEİG, 2015). In some regions, for example, during the hazelnut harvest, farmers generally house workers in shelters built for workers in groves. In the Black Sea region, where ethnic conflict and social hostility towards different ethnic identities are high, workers of Kurdish origin can stay in the orchards away from others, thereby avoiding potential conflicts. In the apricot harvest, workers are accommodated in tents set up in orchards, so that

Figure 6.2 A worker camp site. Source: Development Workshop Archive.

they can cover up the apricots laid out for drying quickly should it rain. The provision of shelter within orchards results in longer working hours and the blurring of the line between work and leisure (Figure 6.2).

Since migrant seasonal agricultural workers are typically allowed to build tents near drainage canals and main roads, both children and adults are at risk of drowning and traffic accidents. Seasonal workers usually reside in tent settlements scattered around farms and villages in isolated places. A Support to Life Association study regarding shelter conditions of migrant seasonal agricultural workers contains striking findings. While as much as 81 per cent of workers are sheltered in tents, only 9 per cent live in permanent structures. A tent is a poorly protected form of shelter that is open on all sides. The report states that the average size of tents is 16 square metres and on average each tent accommodates seven people. While labourers are expected to provide their own shelter, in some regions workers and their families reside in temporary accommodation camps established by the authorities.

Seasonal worker tent settlements resemble a residential neighbourhood and though they vary in size, an average-sized settlement has thirty to fifty tents. Some families pitch two tents next to each other for different purposes:

one tent as a kitchen and one as the living area. In this single-room tent shelter, the whole family eats, sleeps and rests together. All the items that the family has, such as a TV, clothes, beds and bedding, are stored in this area. Because of the tight quarters, children spend all of their time outside the tent, except when they watch TV, sleep or eat. Therefore, it is not surprising that visitors to these tent settlements are first greeted by a large group of children.

Since most tents are pitched on bare ground, it is impossible to protect belongings when it rains heavily; tents easily become flooded. Tents are made from nylon and tarp, making life difficult during the winter when it is cold and windy. During high winds or storms, the tents can easily blow away, so ropes are typically tied to sacks full of stones and placed over the nylon and tarp on the top of the tent. During the summer, on the other hand, the inside of the tent becomes like a greenhouse: extremely hot and humid. On the treeless open fields of the Adana Plain, dust particles, insects, rats, scorpions and snakes enter freely into the tents.

Although the tents are generally positioned to ensure a minimum degree of privacy from the surrounding tents in the area, when the camps are established on river or canal banks, there is no other option but to form tight rows of tents in a small area. Electricity is vital for the inhabitants. During the winter, electricity is used for heating purposes and in the summer to cool off. With electricity food can be refrigerated and kept fresh longer. Potable and utility water comes from tankers in most tent settlements. Some settlements have tap water.

Bonded labour through isolation and confinement

Worker teams of mostly family members and relatives live in isolated and designated tent settlements. Therefore, a highly mobile workforce is kept quite immobile for a certain time period with limited contact with people from outside the tent community. Their basic needs – foodstuff and other necessities – are usually met by labour intermediaries. One of the male workers (twenty-nine years old and father of three children) described life in designated areas:

> *Dayıbaşı* [labour intermediaries] took us here. We are almost 10 families from the same village in Syria. After we arrived in Turkey, we were told that there is work in Adana. A *dayıbaşı* from Urfa took us here and we set our tents near these fields next to the village. We are so far from the city and not

allowed to go to the villages. We cannot move out of this area as the only person with a car is a *dayıbaşı*. This place is too far from everywhere when we get sick and call an ambulance it does not come here. One time, we called it many times but it did not appear at all.

Moving to a designated agricultural tent settlement obliges the whole team to work there. A Syrian worker (thirty-eight years old, father of six children) explained their situation:

We are obliged to work here as there are no other jobs available. Only this work. Tell me where we can go and what we can do. It is only the job we are offered by the dayıbaşı. Now we work for a farmer who owns large orange farms in this area. His products are exported to Europe and Russia and very big business he owns. We mostly work for him and live in this tent area provided by him. We stay here almost six months a year.

Living in isolated tent settlements increase workers' dependence on labour intermediaries due to high immobility. It also bonds workers to remain in the team of a specific labour intermediary as no other opportunities to work and live is available for them (Figure 6.3).

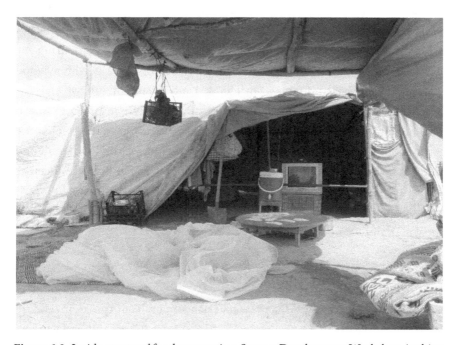

Figure 6.3 Inside a tent and food preparation. Source: Development Workshop Archive.

128   Syrian Refugees and Agriculture in Turkey

Figure 6.4 Young children having a nap in a tent. Source: Development Workshop Archive.

Although tent settlements are confining, they are a cheaper option for Syrian refugees than high rents in city centres. The arrival of a large number of Syrian refugees in such provinces as Mersin and Adana within a short time frame has made their accommodation a significant problem in the region. During my interviews, it was mentioned that flats in Adana's Doğankent neighbourhood are rented out to Syrians for between TRY 400 and 500 per month, which is the double of other rentals to Turkish people. Thus, many Syrians prefer to stay in tent areas or in the accommodations provided by employers in the greenhouse production. In the province of Mersin, a popular destination of greenhouse production, workers are given a living space in which families live together and are from time to time provided with basic food staples by their employers. In the province of Adana, Syrian agricultural workers remain in tents during the winter and summer (Figure 6.4).

Accessing health-care services

Migrant seasonal agricultural workers experience many health problems and are at risk of fatal accidents. For example, in 2014, at least 309 agricultural workers died on the job (KEİG, 2015). Workers are directly exposed to agricultural chemicals. Among health problems, the most common are dizziness, fatigue, back pain, diarrhoea, respiratory infections, dermatological ailments (such as wounds, boils, eczema, scabies and lice), sunstroke, headaches, poisoning, anxiety, depression and suicide attempts (KEİG, 2015). Despite the high incidence of health problems, the distance between places of shelter and medical centres limits access to health care. Furthermore, as migrant seasonal agricultural workers are on the move for around eight months of the year, their access to preventive health care is precarious. As informal employees, they also lack social security coverage, which likewise precludes them from accessing health-care services.

Isolation in tent settlements significantly affects access to health-care services. The barriers pertaining to Syrians' access to primary and secondary health-care systems[5] in Turkey are mainly internal mobility and isolation in rural tent settlements. When Syrians move to cities other than their initial registration place without official permission, they lose access to health-care services. The most frequent health-care need is for newborn infants and children, pregnant women and injured workers due to workplace accidents requiring emergency treatment. Seldomly, secondary health-care services, such as surgeries, are received, and preventive health-care services are never required or benefitted from. Protective health-care services are only in the form of vaccination of infants and basic care for newborns by public health institutions. In fact, prenatal care, family planning, diagnosis of disabilities, infectious diseases, protection of public health, food safety and nutritional health awareness are the health issues requiring the most urgent attention in these locations. However, access to these types of health-care services is quite difficult for households residing in remote locations with limited transportation and financial means.

The story of a fifty-six-year-old Turkmen woman, Hatice, who migrated from her village near Aleppo to Adana with her three daughters and five sons in 2015, is telling in this regard. Her grandfather is from Bilecik, Turkey, one of the Tosun family. She speaks Arabic, Kurdish and Turkish fluently, but her children only speak Arabic, which is a major barrier that prevents them from receiving health care. She notes that they only go to the hospital when they are ill, but they encounter difficulties in the hospital as there are few or no interpreters available. She claims that health-care personnel do not accept Syrians, or they are simply evasive and negligent. As a result, they do not go to hospitals or clinics unless they are gravely ill. One of her daughters is severely disabled and requires hospitalization. Another daughter is also disabled, but she stays with them in the tent. Hatice says they try to take care of her, but they know the care is inadequate. She is in critical condition but they are unable to do much to help her, so they almost leave her for dead. Some mobile health-care teams came to the settlement to offer vaccinations, but when she showed them her disabled daughter, they did nothing for her. As a result, she has no confidence in the health-care system.

The women I interviewed complained about their limited access to health care. When I asked whether they benefit from any health-care services, they typically answer that services are usually limited to natal care and birth. A labour intermediary in a tent camp said that 'When we are about to give birth, we call an ambulance, it takes us to the hospital and we give birth there'. They do not receive any prenatal care or see a doctor before giving birth. One of the reasons for limited access to health-care services is that 'There are no Arabic interpreters in hospitals. Language is a big barrier.' A woman (fifty-five years old and grandmother) also stated that 'We heard that we need to get new identity cards to get social aid, but we do not know where and how to apply for aid', indicating an obvious need for information and guidance to obtain full access to health care. Some women mentioned that they take their children to Syrian doctors and pay as little as TRY 20 for a visit. The informal information networks are an important check-and-balance system. One woman mentioned that they go to Syrian doctors who were also well-known medical personnel back in Syria, and they usually rely on the recommendations of relatives and friends. In the absence of effective access to health-care service, Syrians turn to Syrian doctors who are mostly unregistered and operate illegally in Turkey.

Conclusion

The 3R work regime in seasonal farm work has been a way to include the most vulnerable labour forms and to keep that labour bonded. The 3R regime – based on concentrating labour in isolated tent camps, distributing workers' wages irregularly and depending on labour intermediators for recruitment – has led to a generation of bonded workers in Turkey's seasonal agricultural labour markets. The tighter the hold on labour, the more the control exercised to extract surplus from labour.

While the role of intermediaries in agriculture is significant for recruiting workers and organizing agricultural labour markets, the way they practise their role sometimes ends up generating a bonded, docile and cheap workforce that is sought after in Turkish agricultural production. The need for bonded labour is mostly associated with the natural cycle of production in agriculture and the hunger of the sector to tap into the cheapest forms of labour that may end up requiring the immobility of a mobile labour force – namely, seasonal workers.

Worker retention is sustained through their confinement to isolated tent settlements in deserted rural areas with limited access to alternative job opportunities and city centres, whereas remuneration is practised in a web of complex relations established between labour intermediaries, farmers and workers in which cash payment is circulated only occasionally.

Overall, the 3Rs create a setting in which workers are bonded to agricultural work and a specific intermediary for a season. By limiting workers' physical movement and cutting their access to cash income, this system binds workers to a specific site for a certain time. Further, it enables easy control of labour not only in the realm of production but also in the realm of social reproduction and day-to-day activities of workers. The organization of seasonal work is an umbrella that stretches over all aspects of worker families' lives.

7

Conclusion

Syrian Refugees and Agricultural in Turkey: Work, Precarity and Survival began with two central questions: What is the nature of precarization of Syrian refugee labour in Turkey's seasonal agricultural labour market, and how has women's and children's labour played a central role in the precarization of Syrians in a work regime that continuously seeks paths to bond labour? The increasing dominance of Syrian workers in seasonal agricultural work in Turkey has contributed to making that work highly precarious. Therefore, my aim has been to show the strategies adopted both by the labour supply dynamics that translate into the deployment of the most vulnerable labour forms and by the labour demand that endlessly pursue cheap labour forms and keep labour bonded.

The overall aim of my research was to analyse the precarization of Syrian refugees' labour by highlighting the strategies of labour market actors – workers, employers, intermediaries and market forces. I argued that the precarization of Syrian labour in the Turkish agricultural sector has been widely influenced by intersecting vulnerabilities put into play to have access to agricultural jobs and by the labour recruitment and retention strategies deployed. Empirical data highlight that supply- and demand-side strategies have developed simultaneously to ensure access to jobs. For instance, Syrian families have supplied labour by using more and more children and women to bargain down to lower wage levels in the midst of severe economic necessity and survival, while the agricultural sector has adopted such organizational strategies as isolated tent settlements, labour intermediaries and a specific wage payment system to fulfil its needs. By looking at the intersection of these two sets of factors, demand and supply, I show that differential inclusion of migrant labour based on gender, ethnicity, age and patriarchal relations also supports the precarization of Syrian labour by increasing the bargaining power of migrant labour, namely the domestic native Turkish precariat.

This research was located within a specific line of literature that draws heavily on interrelationships between immigrant labour and a context-specific work regime that is based on the integration of intersectional vulnerabilities (Waite, 2009, Mezzadra and Nielsen, 2013, Crenshaw, 1991, Federici, 2008, Mezzadri, 2020). The literature demonstrates that this precarization has been highly feminized by the integration of social reproduction into the realm of production and the precarization of 'life-worlds' of migrants, both of which do not help women change their subordinate positions in their families and communities. Schierup and Jørgensen (2016) show that immigrants, regarded as a surplus population reaching multiple millions, are a global reserve army, at the disposal of transnational corporations, sub-contractors and franchises (Schierup and Jørgensen, 2016). Women have been the most important component of this global reserve army; their labour is considered to be essential for maintaining a fresh labour supply in global labour markets (Portes and Sassen-Koob, 1987; Weeks, 2011). It is also significant to emphasize that the utilization of social structures that enable subordinate female labour under patriarchal control is practised within specific contexts, which is what Harvey (1982) calls as spatial fixes, in which the contestation between capital and labour is concrete and embedded as it is realized in a specific labour process, even though the global capital acts on a transnational space and can be highly abstract.

A close examination of Syrian refugees' work in Turkey's seasonal agriculture sector shows that the precarization of Syrian labour is generated through a set of strategies applied in the agricultural sector through the integration of the most vulnerable labour force – women and children – and the sector's labour demand strategies – recruitment, retention and remuneration – such as the use of labour intermediaries, secluded refugee settlements and the wage payment system. By focusing on intersectional vulnerabilities and context-dependent precarization in exploring the labour market integration of Syrian refugees, the book shows that differential inclusion of migrant labour through gender, ethnicity, age and patriarchal relations could also support the precarization of Syrian labour by increasing the bargaining power of migrant labour, namely the domestic, native Turkish precariat. It also has shown that immigrant women are not only a source of cheap and docile labour but also agents who directly supply competitive and low-cost supply with their role in the realms of social production, an indispensable part of agricultural seasonal work. The empirical sections of the book have documented the ways context-dependent strategies absorb and generate precarious workers and Syrian refugee work in Turkey's agricultural sector, which is a highly global industry producing for world markets.

Precarization of Syrian labour in Turkey's agricultural sector

The first objective of the book was to explore the nature of Syrian refugees' work and help to render it visible in Turkey's seasonal agricultural labour markets, where most of the work takes place informally with no official recording. In recent years, Syrian refugees have been a major supplier of informal labour in Turkey's many labour-intensive sectors, such as agriculture, textile, construction and services. Turkey has been home to the largest Syrian refugee community in the world, and the overwhelming majority of refugees live outside camps and struggle to make a living. The young and family-based composition of the Syrian population differs from the trends appearing in the overall refugee movement to Europe, which is male-dominated. Syrians are largely relegated to informal jobs at low wages, with limited access to legal protections.

The agricultural sector has been one of the major work opportunities for Syrian immigrants since the early days of their arrival in 2011. Relying on wage labour has been the response of smallholders in Turkey's agricultural sector to the changing social and economic structure in recent years. Seasonal farmworkers in Turkey did not become a significant and noticeable phenomenon until the mid-1990s, when internal conflict erupted in the south-eastern region of the country and resulted in the evacuation of Kurdish villages. Later in the 2000s, seasonal work has turned to hosting diverse workers' groups from different ethnic backgrounds. The source of agricultural labour is extensively diversified as many worker groups coming from different backgrounds have been competing for agricultural jobs. The analysis in Chapter 3 emphasized that while the migrant labour from Syria, Azerbaijan and Georgia has been important for the precarization of Turkish seasonal agricultural workforce, this trend is enforced through the cultivation of antagonistic relations between different segments of agricultural wage workers and rivalry of the poor.

The precarization of Syrian refugees has been based on the rivalry between different workers trying to capture work opportunities in agricultural production. This competition ends with worsening working conditions and downward spiralling daily wages. Travelling with all families together from one site to another year-round and living in tent settlements are the most peculiar characteristics of seasonal agricultural work in which working relations are organized by the regulatory authority of labour intermediaries. Working up to twelve hours a day under extreme weather conditions and living in inadequate shelters in isolated locations, Syrians struggle to make ends meet in Turkey's fertile lands. They are highly mobile, moving from one province to another, to meet the demands of seasonal farm work and form work teams composed of ten to fifteen people, mostly based on familial relations and kin networks.

The book has shown that the degree of ultra-exploitation, coupled with harsh working conditions in agricultural work, shaped under extreme competition taking place between worker groups, leads to refugees deploying strategies to find ways to cope with deteriorating working conditions. The most common response is to rely more and more on children's and women's work and labour to survive, indicating precarization through intersecting vulnerabilities. In this regard, the role of women in the realm of social reproduction emerges as vital for survival and is highly linked to the ability of Syrians to offer their labour to capitalist production at lower and lower prices. In the seasonal agricultural work, the 'Syrian' means cheap, reliable and docile labour that is ready to work for long hours for very small returns and mostly on informal terms in a sector that is continuously seeking ways to bond and limits the mobility and options of workers. The vulnerability of refugees living in the margins of rural Turkey promises a successful agricultural sector only in extreme exploitation of labour and communal sacrifice for very small returns and marginal incomes.

Existing conditions of legal rights available to Syrians and the labour markets built up two different pathways of integration for Syrian refugees that have the main axis of precarization of Syrian labour in Turkey. One is formal integration, through which refugees are able to make claims to citizenship rights, as well as negotiating their access to employment, humanitarian assistance and social services. The second is precarious, informal integration, in which Syrians are becoming an indispensable part of labour-intensive industries through which Turkey enters the global international competition in a constant search of tapping into the cheaper forms of labour.

The book has discussed increasing tension and conflict between different groups of poor people competing for the same jobs; this competition is a process of precarization in seasonal farm work in Turkey. Syrians have mostly lost their access to formal education in the post-migration process; therefore, their chances of breaking the cycle of poverty are slim. Keeping in mind the scarcity and even absence of financial resources, specifically income-generating activities of Syrian refugees in Turkey, due to the limitations of their temporary protection status, access to formal, better paid and permanent jobs seems the only solution to mitigate this risk of poverty and marginalization in the first place. However, such a causal dilemma makes it hard to resolve.

Intersecting vulnerabilities and precarization: Women and children

The second objective of this research was to examine the supply factors that condition Syrians' work and labour in seasonal agricultural work and the supply strategies of precarization of immigrant labour. After the sudden arrival of Syrian refugees to Turkey in 2011, they began to compete in the labour market to get informal job opportunities and the best way to do it has been to work for lower prices. The seasonal agricultural work has been one of these jobs for which the Syrians needed to compete to get a grab. The integration of Syrians into agricultural work is largely based on a string of absorption strategies adopted both by refugees competing to access these jobs – supply-side strategies – and by the sector seeking to integrate the most vulnerable labour force. The supply-side strategies of Syrian refugees have been constructed to win the rivalry taking place between poverty-stricken groups to get agricultural jobs and have resulted in the deployment of the most vulnerable segments of the Syrian population, namely women and children. Infinite capacity to control women's and child labour is an important aspect of the seasonal agricultural labour market, and control over workers, takes many shapes, handed over from the heads of households to labour intermediaries and then to landowner employers.

The book has discussed how the intersecting vulnerabilities of the Syrian community have enacted in the extensive use of female and child labour in agricultural seasonal work. Syrian women's work in agriculture production has increased dramatically after their replacement in Turkey. For many, this has been the first experience of participating in income-generating activities and starting work in the fields. The presence of a high number of Syrian women in Turkey's agricultural sector can well be evaluated as a face of feminization of agricultural production. The feminization of agricultural production has gone hand in hand with strict patriarchal control exercised over women and their dependent role on the hierarchical chain of paternal relations. Chapter 5 has argued in the case of Syrian women's work that feminization is not only about increasing the number of women in paid work but is also disguised in the discourses of who is the best worker. It also supports the arguments that the world of women's work has been the bearer of gender hierarchies and a gendered division of labour in employment. Patriarchal structures in culture, society, markets and corporations have kept women within the confines of particular activities in the informal economy, thereby hindering women's financial and social gains through their paid work.

Syrian women's activities taking place in the realm of social reproduction is as vital for seasonal agricultural work as the activities done in the fields and farms. Worker families moving from one province to another altogether, carrying all their household stuff to construct a home in a tent camp, means mobilizing women's reproductive labour to care for families and at the same time to release their labour for work in the fields. It also enables workers to live on cheaper terms that in turns result in lower wage levels. The migration process has increased not only women's time spent in agricultural production but also the time spent doing domestic chores and caring activities. This is mostly due to living in a tent settlement. Migrant women have to spend more time and greater effort to reorganize life in temporary and non-standard shelters and devote more time for the care needs of family members and for other household chores. The heavy burden shouldered by women in harsher living conditions results in a division of labour between different women members of families, as the younger ones do agricultural work and the older ones stay at home and do the domestic tasks.

Intersectional vulnerabilities of Syrian women have manifested themselves in the degree of control exercised over their labour and work. Women at work are strictly observed and controlled by a performance system that works as a system of discipline and surveillance. In the system, the working speed is set by a foreman who dictates workers by 'shouting out', whose authority over women and girls is more powerful than that of men and boys. Disciplining workers with the authority of man is the main reason for employing women and children in seasonal farm work. Women are not only preferred as workers because of their hard work and 'God-given' skills of agricultural work but also because of the degree of control that can be exercised over women's labour and income generated in agricultural work. Thus, women's earnings are directly paid to their heads of households, mostly their fathers or husbands. The diffusion of patriarchal control over women's labour and earning is related to familial-based nature of worker teams composed where women work together with other close family members and relatives. Male heads of households and labour contractors form an ally to decide who would work from a specific family. Their collaboration also extends to control the income generated. As a result, it is not surprising to see that women's earnings are paid to male heads of households. As a result, women who are never paid the wages they earn and do not have control over their cash income are made dependent upon their fathers or husbands for their personal needs and expenses – if women could even be considered to have any personal spending and needs.

The Chapter 5 focuses on the extent of child labour in Syrian households, the perceptions of child labour and how child labour is justified by families, labour intermediaries and farmers. By and large, it shows that children's work in agriculture is instrumental for families to reach out and grab precarious jobs and for farmers to tap into cheaper labour forms. Syrian child workers have fewer opportunities in education and alternatives available to them to break away from hard labour in agriculture but are in a destitute situation to submit to hard-working conditions as the new precariat of Turkey. The prevalence of child labour in the agricultural sector, which worsens with the influx of Syrians, is justified mostly with poverty and as a way of survival for many families. When directed with the question of *why children become workers*, the most common response is the struggle to meet ends and poverty mostly generated as a result of migration. In seasonal agricultural production, the chief survival strategy of Syrian households is to direct as many members as possible to income-generating activities. Children come to be quite useful in the process. Since the number of people living in Syrian households is high, more people are put into work to bring in more income, through which survival is secured. The intersecting vulnerabilities embedded in child labour in Turkey's agricultural sector are illustrated in the following testimonies that show how Syrians justify their children's engagement under harsh working conditions.

The winning ticket of Syrian refugees is to tap into the large pool of women and children whose labour is essential for production in the fields but also enable social reproduction of workers families. Departing from these findings, the book dwells on the concepts of 'differential inclusion' (Mezzadra and Nielsen, 2013: 165), which refers to the role of border in selecting, filtering and differentiating migrant labour and to the inclusion of segments of migrants from different levels of subordination and heterogeneity that shape labour markets and intersectional vulnerabilities, as a form of embodiments of interconnected disadvantages based on social categorizations such as race, ethnicity, class, gender and social status such as being migrants. This concept of vulnerable integration is used to refer to the inclusion of the most vulnerable segments of migrant labour in the face of rivalry taking place among different segments of the precariat to grab the existing jobs in the Turkish agricultural labour market. This sets the basis of an analysis in which the international migration as a form of double movement and agency is an integral part of social transformations but in return affects the ways in which the global social transformations played out in national, local, household and individual levels by adopting Polanyi's concept of 'double movement' as agency through which people develop varying forms of agency and resistance. My objective is, therefore, to analyse how women and child labour is utilized in seasonal agricultural work and why the refugee families rely more and more on these two categories of labour to have access to agricultural jobs, which is also supported by the role women and children play in social reproduction of their families and communities.

Bonding refugee labour and precarization

The third objective of the book was to provide an understanding of the labour demand strategies conditioning Syrian refugees' entry into agricultural wage work in Turkey. Isolated tent settlements (retention), labour intermediaries (recruitment) and the wage payment system (remuneration) are the most distinctive strategies the sector has adopted to organize the labour process. The split in the agricultural workforce as non-migrants and migrants has led to the widening of precarization strategies adopted by both sides of labour supply and demand through which migrant labour is rendered more vulnerable, more flexible and more competitive and espoused to the unfree labour demands of Turkish seasonal agricultural labour markets. These strategies reveal the broader interrelated structural process in which both structure and agency play a crucial role in reproducing, challenging and reconstructing the power relations in the labour market. The utilization of migrant labour in agricultural production has been a way of transnational connectedness that affects national societies, local communities and individuals in a way of social expression of global connections and processes (Castells, 2015).

The seasonal agricultural work in Turkey rests upon a specific work regime in which the agricultural labour market constantly tries to include the most vulnerable labour forms and keep that labour bonded. In the sector, the practices of recruitment, retention and remuneration (3R) of labour can clearly be identified as a form of bonding labour to seasonal farm work for a certain period of time. The combination of the 3R represents a powerful labour management regime, which Turkey's agricultural sector is currently using to fuel its integration with the world economy and lower the cost of food production for the whole population. This system secures that labour costs are low, the productivity of workers is high, and there is access to extensive low-cost labour reserves. Further, the form of labour capture in the 3R work regime allows access to cheap labour without a longer-term build-up of labour institutions that would lead to better working conditions and labour solidarities. Rather, the systemic working of the 3Rs regime is based on concentrating labour in isolated tent camps, retaining workers' wages, and the role of labour intermediation has led to a generation of bonded labour regime in Turkey's seasonal agricultural labour markets.

The 3Rs labour regime in seasonal agricultural work is based on the role of labour intermediaries in recruitment, remuneration and retention of labour in tent settlements. Since the seasonal agricultural labour markets work differently on these regards than those of other labour markets, labour intermediaries are central in the functioning of the 3Rs. As the role of intermediaries is a far stretch beyond recruitment, they are active agents in determining the organization of retention and remuneration of agricultural workers. The retention of workers is sustained through their confinement to isolated tent settlements in deserted rural areas with limited access to alternative job opportunities and city centres, whereas the remuneration is practised in a web of complex relations established between labour intermediaries, farmers and workers in which from time to time no cash payment is circulated. Overall, the 3Rs function to create a setting in which workers are bonded to agricultural work and a specific intermediary for a season.

The 3R work regime in seasonal farm work has been a way of including the most vulnerable labour forms and to keep that labour bonded. The sector-specific operation of recruitment, remuneration and retention is examined in this chapter to bond Syrian agricultural workers. It has shown that the systemic working of the 3Rs regime is based on concentrating labour in isolated tent camps, retaining workers' wages, and the role of labour intermediation has led to a generation of bonded labour regime in Turkey's seasonal agricultural labour markets. The tighter the bondage on labour, the more the control exercised to extract surplus from labour. The ultimate control over refugee labour in Turkey's agricultural sector is secured through the operation of work regime based on the 3Rs.

The organizational role of labour intermediaries not only remains in the realm of matching workers with jobs but also extends to the regulation of workers' access to cash income and their tent settlement. Workers retained through their confinement to isolated tent settlements in deserted rural areas. This has limited their reach to alternative job opportunities and city centres. In addition, the remuneration practices established in a web of complex relations between labour intermediaries, farmers and workers is used as a way of retaining workers. Labour intermediaries are of critical importance in the organization of agricultural labour force and hold the power of delivering the wages to workers. Therefore, they stand at the heart of agricultural job markets and use their power to keep workers dependent on them. The intermediaries have generated their own way of paying workers without using cash income at all. If one considers the fact that an intermediary can control over forty to forty-five people in the smallest scale, the total income managed by an intermediary is quite large.

Overall, the 3Rs work regime functions to create a setting in which workers are bonded to agricultural work and a specific intermediary for a season. This is, in a sense, the context-specific and organic way to expropriate surplus and organize labour force control. By limiting the physical movement and cutting workers' access to cash income, agricultural labour is kept bonded to a specific location for a certain time. This system secures that labour costs kept at the lowest level but the productivity of workers is high by ensuring access to extensive low-cost labour reserves. Further, it enables an easy control of labour not only in the realm of production but also in the realm of social reproduction and day-to-day activities of workers. The organization of seasonal work is an umbrella that stretches over all aspects of the lives of worker families.

The bonding labour in Turkey's seasonal farm work is the context-specific organic way to expropriate surplus. The seasonal agricultural work regime is geared to bonding labour at a specific location and work, not only through linking productive and reproductive labour but also through limiting the physical movement of labour by confining them to certain places and jobs. To explore how the 3Rs labour regime works in Turkey's seasonal agricultural labour markets, this chapter provides an analysis of the three separate areas of recruitment, retention and remuneration and the ways in which they function to bond workers and exploit labour.

Notes

Chapter 1

1 Karl Polanyi argued in *The Great Transformation* (2001) that the development of market societies over the past 200 years has been shaped by a double movement. On one side is the movement of laissez faire – the efforts by a variety of groups to expand the scope and influence of self-regulating markets. On the other side has been the movement of protection – the initiatives, again by a wide range of social actors, to insulate the fabric of social life from the destructive impact of market pressures. The double movement idea elaborates the micro-foundations of the protective counter movement to explain how agents sometimes have the opportunity, the power and the capacity to challenge and change the institutional structures of market societies.

2 I also utilized the findings of a 2016 research conducted by Development Workshop in the Adana province with 266 Syrian refugee households that produced information for 1,655 individuals (Development Workshop 2016) and a face-to-face interview was conducted with 141 labour intermediaries living and working in Şanlıurfa and Adana (Development Workshop 2018). The second project tackled the question of how different remuneration types (daily, piece rate, monthly or seasonal) affect child labour use in agricultural production. Fieldwork was conducted between July and September 2017 in the provinces of Adana, Eskişehir, Giresun, Konya, Mersin, Ordu and Şanlıurfa, where most agricultural workers are employed seasonally on different corps.

3 The survey was applied by the Adana staff of Development Workshop (DW) Cooperative, which is an NGO working for the elimination of child labour in seasonal agricultural production in Turkey and has long years of experience in the province of Adana. The DW has been active working among Syrian refugees in Adana and has a database for their settlements in tent areas.

4 The number of women was 453 and men 452 in the sample. The distribution of population in age group is as follows: 0–5-year-olds, 13.6 per cent; 6–14, 30.5 per cent; 15–17, 15.1 per cent; 18–21, 12 per cent; 22–29, 7.7 per cent; 30–39, 7.3 per cent; 40–49, 7.6 per cent, and over 50 years and older 6.1 per cent.

5   The term includes a number of well-defined legal categories of people, such as migrant workers; persons whose particular types of movements are legally defined, such as smuggled migrants; as well as those whose status or means of movement are not specifically defined under international law, such as international students (IOM 2019).

Chapter 2

1   Although outlawed by the United Nations Supplementary Convention on the Abolition of Slavery, the Slave Trade and Institutions and Practices Similar to Slavery (1956), this form of labour is still widely practised in some parts of the world.

Chapter 3

1   The most widely known programme is Canada's The Seasonal Agricultural Workers Programme (SAWP).
2   In 1907, 81 per cent of the land was divided into 50-acre plots on average; a family of four or five was sufficient to process land of this size. As of 1909, the average farm size in western Anatolia was about 25 acres (Kasaba, 1993: 56–7).
3   Of the total $184.5 million supplied between the years 1948 and 1952, $38.282 million was reserved for the agricultural sector. In addition to bringing a high performance to the sector in general, the aids brought about a number of significant contributions such as agricultural mechanization, the farmers taking over the modern agricultural production techniques, the enlargement of farmlands and enhancement of agricultural production. Between 1948 and 1953, the economic development relied heavily on the agricultural sector. While the proportion of agricultural sector in gross national product was 38.4 per cent in 1947, it rose to 45 per cent in 1953. On average, Turkish Economy grew by 11 per cent between 1950 and 1953 per year. At the same period, thanks to the developments in the agricultural sector, the per capita income increased at a rate of 28 per cent (Özer 2014).
4   Imece refers to a kind of a mutual agricultural work that is organized by small agricultural producers. All seasonal family-farm harvest work follows a prescribed pattern. Household members in a village work without pay in the fields of their neighbours during harvest. During the 1990s, this system dissolved

due to a lack of unpaid family members following the accelerated urbanization process.

5 *Icar* corresponds to sharecropping, a form of agriculture in which a landowner allows a tenant to use land in return for a share of the crops produced on their portion of the land; the portion is usually 50 per cent in Turkey.

6 Kavalali Ibrahim Pasha (1789, Kavala – 10 November 1848, Kahire) was the local governor (wali) of Egypt and Syria.

7 Çukurova is a region in southern Turkey and includes the provinces of Mersin, Adana, Osmaniye and Hatay. The majority of the region consists of plains, one of which is the Adana Plain. Even though the names Adana Plain (Adana Ovası) and Çukurova are generally used interchangeably, it is a common mistake. Adana Plain is only a part of the larger region called Çukurova, located to the south of the city of Adana, including the Seyhan, Karataş, Yüreğir and Yumurtalık districts.

8 In 2017, Georgians were kept exempt from getting work permits as long as they were registered in local provincial government offices and stayed to work in agriculture. However, most still work in agriculture without registration and enter Turkey with tourist visas.

9 IOM defines irregular migration – movement of persons that takes place outside the laws, regulations or international agreements governing the entry into or exit from the state of origin, transit or destination.

Chapter 4

1 The number was 13,290 in 2016, 20,966 in 2017 and 34,573 in 2018.
2 The average monthly wage of Syrian men was TRY 1,337 and TRY 1,083 for Syrian women in 2017 (ILO Ankara Office 2020).
3 During the time of data collection in July 2016, the USD was around TRY3 and Euros TRY3,2.

Chapter 5

1 The Turkish Labour Law of 2003 establishes a forty-five-hour workweek. But OECD data shows that the average worked hours a week usually exceeds forty-five. The highest was 50.9 hours in 2009 and then fall down to 47.7 hours in 2017, which is still the highest in EU countries (OECD 2019).

2 The minimum wage in July 2017 was TRY 1.777 before tax. USD in July 2017 was TRY 3.5.
3 Article 71 also regulates employment hours for children, allowing ten hours or fewer per week for children continuing their education. Children who have finished compulsory education and are not actively engaged in an educational programme can work up to thirty-five hours per week. For children aged fifteen to eighteen, the work week is extended to forty hours.
4 The most recent data on child labour in Turkey was collected by TURKSTAT in 2012. The results of the 2012 Child Labour Force Survey show that 893,000 children between the ages of six and seventeen worked in Turkey, comprising 5.9 per cent of all children and 15.6 per cent of all children in that age group.
5 The total number of children in the sample is 451 and 329, corresponding to a rate of 72.9 per cent.

Chapter 6

1 According to the results of the *Statistics on Family, Address-Based Population Registration System in 2016 Report (ABPRS)* published by TURKSTAT on 10 May 2017, the average size of households in Turkey was 3.5 individuals.
2 Directive on Employment Intermediation in Agriculture art. 9.
3 In all these different wage systems, workers are paid with a wage care when they complete the work.
4 *Kürekçi* is a local sharecropping practised in cotton production in the province of Şanlıurfa in which the cropper takes one-third of the total harvest.
5 Primary health services are at home or outpatient treatment and are primarily provided by small-scale health-care facilities accepting no in-patients. There are three main institutions providing primary health care: Family Health Centers, Public Health Centers and 112 Emergency Health Services. Secondary health services include in-patient care in hospitals. Tertiary health services include in-patient care that specializes, depending on gender, age group or disease, generally with proper specialized equipment and personnel. These services are usually provided by specialized hospitals or teaching hospitals (Ministry of Health, 'Toplum Sağlığı Merkezi ve Bağlı Birimler Yönetmeliğinde Değişiklik', Official Gazette No: 30431).

Bibliography

Acker, J. (2000), 'Revisiting Class', *Social Politics*, 7 (2): 192–214.

Afanasieva, D. (2016), 'In Turkish Sweatshops, Syrian Children Sew to Survive. Reuters Investigates', 26 July. Available online: https://www.reuters.com/investigates/special-report/europe-migrants-turkey-children/ (accessed on 22 February 2020).

Akay, A., A. Constant and C. Giulietti (2014), 'The Impact of Immigration on the Well-Being of Natives', *Journal of Economic Behavior & Organization*, 103: 72–92.

Akdeniz, E. (2014), *Suriye Savaşının Gölgesinde Mülteci Işçiler*, İstanbul: Evrensel Yayınları.

Amnesty International (2014), *Hayatta Kalma Mücadelesi: Türkiye'deki Suriye'den Gelen Mülteciler*, Londra: Amnesty International.

Anderson, B. (2007). 'A Very Private Business: Exploring the Demand for Migrant Domestic Workers', *European Journal of Women's Studies*, 14 (3): 247–64.

Anderson, K. and D. Jack (1991), 'Learning to Listen: Interview Techniques and Analysis', in S. B. Gluck and D. Patai (eds), *Women's Words: The Feminist Practice of Oral History*, 11–26, London: Routledge.

Anthias, F. and N. Y. Davis (1989), 'Introduction', in N. Yuval Davis and F. Anthias (eds), *Woman, Nation, State*, 1–15, Basingstoke: Macmillan.

Arnold, D. and J. R. Bongiovi (2013), 'Precarious, Informalizing, and Flexible Work: Transforming Concepts and Understandings', *American Behavioral Scientist*, 57 (3): 289–308.

Aydın, Z. (2010), 'Neo-Liberal Transformation of Turkish Agriculture', *Journal of Agrarian Change*, 10 (2): 149–87.

Baban, F., S. Ilcan and K. Rygiel (2017), 'Syrian Refugees in Turkey: Pathways to Precarity, Differential Inclusion, and Negotiated Citizenship Rights', *Journal of Ethnic and Migration Studies*, 43 (1): 1–17.

Bakker, I. and S. Gill (2003a), 'Global Political Economy and Social Reproduction', in I. Bakker and S. Gill (eds), *Power, Production and Social Reproduction: Human In/security in the Global Political Economy*, 3–16, New York: Palgrave Macmillan.

Bakker, I. and S. Gill (2003b), 'Ontology, Method, and Hypotheses', in I. Bakker and S. Gill (eds), *Power, Production and Social Reproduction: Human In/security in the Global Political Economy*, 17–41, New York: Palgrave Macmillan.

Banaji, J. (2010), *Theory as History: Essays on Modes of Production and Exploitation*, Leiden and Boston: Brill.

Badurashvili, I. (2012), 'The Socio-Political Impact of Labour Migration on Georgia', CARIM-East Research Report 2012/21, European University Institute, Robert Schuman Centre for Advanced Studies.

Bahadur, G. (2014), *Coolie Woman: The Odyssey of Indenture*, Chicago: University of Chicago Press.

Barrientos, S. M. (2011), 'Labour Chains: Analysing the Role of Labour Contractors in Global Production Networks', The University of Manchester, Brooks World Poverty Institute, 11 July. Available online: www.capturingthegains.org/pdf/bwpi-wp-15311.pdf (accessed on 10 January 2020).

Basok, T. (2003), 'Mexican Seasonal Migration to Canada and Development: A Community-Based Comparison', *International Migration*, 41 (2): 3–26.

Bauder, H (2006), *Labor Movement: How Migration Regulates Labor Markets*, New York: Oxford University Press.

Bauder, H. (2014), 'Domicile Citizenship, Human Mobility and Territoriality', *Progress in Human Geography*, 38 (1): 91–106.

Beneria, L. and M. Roldan (1987), *The Crossroads of Class and Gender: Industrial Homework, Subcontracting, and Household Dynamics in Mexico City*, Chicago: University of Chicago Press.

Bernstein, H. (2010), *Class Dynamics of Agrarian Change*, Halifax and Winnipeg: Fernwood.

Bohning, W. R. (1984), *Studies in International Labour Migration*, London: The Macmillan Press.

Borland, K. (1991), 'That Is Not What I Said: Interpretative Conflict in Oral Narrative Research', in S. B. Gluck and D. Patai (eds), *Women's Words: The Feminist Practice of Oral History*, 63–76, London: Routledge.

Bradley, H. (1996), *Fractured Identities: Changing Patterns of Inequality*, London: Polity Press.

Branch, E. H. and C. Hanley (2011), 'Regional Convergence in Low-Wage Work and Earnings, 1970–2000', *Sociological Perspectives*, 54 (4): 569–92.

BSR (2008), 'International Labour Migration: A Responsible Role for Business', Business for Social Responsibility. Available online: http://www.bsr.org/reports/BSR_LaborMigrationRoleforBusiness.pdf (accessed on 14 March 2020).

Burch, D. and G. Lawrence (2007), 'Supermarkets and Agri-Food Supply Chains', in D. Burch and G. Lawrence (eds), *Transformations in the Production and Consumption of Foods*, 1–28, Cheltenham: Edward Elgar.

Burch, D., J. Dixon and G. Lawrence (2013), 'Introduction to Symposium on the Changing Role of Supermarkets in Global Supply Chains. From Seedling to Supermarket: Agri-Food Supply Chains in Transition', *Agriculture and Human Values*, 30: 215–24.

Campbell, I. and R. Price (2016), 'Precarious Work and Precarious Workers: Towards an Improved Conceptualisation', *Economic and Labour Relations Review*, 27 (3): 314–32.

Carr, M. and M. Alter Chen (2002), 'Globalization and the Informal Economy: How Global Trade and Investment Impact on the Working Poor', Working Paper on the Informal Economy 1, International Labour Organization.

Castles, S. (2015), 'International Human Mobility: Key Issues and Challenges to Social Theory', in S. Castles, D. Ozkul and M. A. Cubas (eds), *Social Transformation and Migration National and Local Experiences in South Korea, Turkey, Mexico and Australia*, Migration, Diasporas and Citizenship Series, 3–14, London and New York: Palgrave.

Castles, S., D. Ozkul and M. A. Cubas (2015), *Social Transformation and Migration National and Local Experiences in South Korea, Turkey, Mexico and Australia*, Migration, Diasporas and Citizenship Series, London and New York: Palgrave.

Castells, M. (2015), *Networks of Outrage and Hope: Social Movements in the Internet Age*, 2nd edn, London: Polity Press.

Centre for Transnational Development and Collaboration (CTDC) (2015), *Syrian Refugees in Turkey: Gender Analysis*, London. http://ctdc.org/content/analysis.pdf (accessed on 03 September 2019).

Ceritoglu, E., H. B. Yunculer, H. Torun and S. Tumen (2017), 'The Impact of Syrian Refugees on Natives' Labor Market Outcomes in Turkey: Evidence from a Quasi-Experimental Design', Working Papers 1705, Research and Monetary Policy Department, Central Bank of the Republic of Turkey.

Chamberlayne, P. and M. Rustin (1999), *From Biography to Social Policy: Final Report of the Sostris Project*, Centre for Biography in Social Policy, Department of Sociology, University of East London. https://cordis.europa.eu/docs/projects/files/SOE/SOE2963010/76095551-6_en.pdf (accessed on 25 July 2020).

Chen, M., J. Vanek, F. Lund and J. Heintz (2005), *Progress of the World's Women: Women, Work, and Poverty*, New York: UNIFEM.

Charles N. and H. Hintjens (1998), *Gender, Ethnicity and Political Ideologies*, London: Routledge.

Crenshaw, K. W. (1991), 'Mapping the Margins: Intersectionality, Identity Politics, and Violence Against Women of Color', *Stanford Law Review*, 43 (6): 1241–99.

Crisan, C. (2007), *Romania Ltd – a Case Study of (I)Responsible Conduct in Human Resources*, (Mimeo). Bucharest: National School for Political and Administrative Studies.

Cockburn, C. (1991), *In the Way of Women: Men's Resistance to Sex Equality in Organizations*, London: Macmillan.

Constant, A. F. (2014), 'Do Migrants Take the Jobs of Native Workers?', *IZA World of Labor* 10: Available online: https://wol.iza.org/uploads/articles/10/pdfs/do-mi grants-take-the-jobs-of-native-workers.pdf (accessed on 19 March 2020).

Constant, A. and K. F. Zimmermann (2005), 'Immigrant Performance and Selective Immigration Policy: a European Perspective', The Institute for the Study of Labor (IZA) Discussion Paper No. 1715.

Council of Europe (1995), 'Immigrant Women and Integration, Community Relations', Directorate of Social and Economic Affairs, 1 March. Available online: http://www.coe.int/t/dg3/migration/archives/Documentation/Series_Commu nity_Relations/Immigrant_women_and_integration_en.pdf (accessed on 14 February 2021).

Corrado, A., C. Castro and D. Perrotta (2017), 'Introduction. Cheap Food, Cheap Labour, High Profits. Agriculture and Mobility in The Mediterranean', in A. Corrado, C. Castro and D. Perrotta (eds), *Migration and Agriculture Mobility and Change in the Mediterranean Area*, 1–24, London and New York: Routledge.

Cupolo, D. (2017), 'Cop-out or Vital Lifeline? Massive EU Cash Aid Programme Rolls Out for Refugees in Turkey', 25 January. Available online: https://www.thenewhu manitarian.org/special-report/2017/01/25/cop-out-or-vital-lifeline-massive-eu-ca sh-aid-programme-rolls-out-refugees (accessed April 2020).

Çalışma ve Sosyal Güvenlik Bakanlığı – Çalışma Genel Müdürlüğü (2017), 'Çocuk İşçiliği ile Mücadele Ulusal Programı 2017–2023'. Available online: https://ailevec alisma.gov.tr/media/1322/cocukisciligimucadele_2017_2023_tr.pdf (accessed on 07 September 2019).

ÇAYSİAD (2015), '2014 Yılı ÇAYSİAD Çay Bölgesi Istihdam Raporu'. Available online: http://www.caysiad.org.tr/index.php?sayfa=2015_yilina_girerken_2014_yi li_cay_bolgesi_istihdam_raporu.45&d=tr (accessed on 25 November 2015).

Çelik, K., Z. Şimşek, Y. Yüce Tar and A. Kırca Duman (2015), *Gezici Mevsimlik Tarım İşinde Çalışan Kadınların Çalışma ve Yaşam Koşullarının İrdelenmesi*, Ankara: Dünya Bankası.

Çetinkaya, Ö. (2008), 'Farm Labour Intermediaries in Seasonal Agricultural Work in Adana, Çukurova', Middle Eastern Technical University, Unpublished MA Thesis, Ankara.

Çınar, S. (2012), 'Bağımlı Çalışma İlişkileri Kapsamında Mevsimlik Tarım İşçilerinin Malatya Örneği Üzerinden Analizi', PhD diss., Marmara University.

Çınar, S. (2014), Öteki "Proleterya": De-Proletarizasyon ve Mevsimlik Tarım İşçileri, Ankara: NotaBene Yayınları.

Davis, K. (2008), 'Intersectionality as Buzzword: A Sociology of Science Perspective on What Makes a Feminist Theory Successful', *Feminist Theory*, 9 (1): 67–85.

Dedeoğlu, S. and Ç. Ekiz Gökmen (2011), *Göç ve Sosyal Dışlanma: Türkiye'de Yabancı Göçmen Kadınlar*, Ankara: Efil Yayınevi.

Dedeoğlu, S. (2012), *Women Workers in Turkey: Global Industrial Production in Istanbul*, London: I.B. Tauris.

Dedeoğlu, S. (2014), *Migrants, Work and Social Integration, Women's Labour in Turkish Ethnic Economy*, Palgrave-MacMillan.

Dedeoğlu, S. (2018), 'Tarımsal Üretimde Göçmen İşçiler: Yoksulluk Nöbetinden Yoksulların Rekabetine', *Çalışma ve Toplum*, 56: 37–68.

De Genova, N. (2002), 'Migrant "Illegality" and Deportability in Everyday Life', *Annual Review of Anthropology*, 31: 419–47.

De Genova, N. and N. Peutz (2010), *The Deportation Regime: Sovereignty, Space, and the Freedom of Movement*, Durham, NC and London: Duke University Press.

Del Carpio, X. and M. Wagner (2015), 'The Impact of Syrians Refugees on the Turkish Labor Market', Policy Research Working Paper No. 7402. World Bank, Washington, DC, August. Available online: https://openknowledge.worldbank.org/handle/10986/22659 License: CC BY 3.0 IGO (accessed on 25 December 2019).

DeVault, M. L. (1996), 'Talking Back to Sociology: Distinctive Contributions of Feminist Methodology', *Annual Review of Sociology*, 22: 29–50.

Development Workshop [Kalkınma Atölyesi] (2014), Fındık Hasadının Oyuncuları: Batı Karadeniz İllerinde Fındık Hasadında Yer Alan Mevsimlik Gezici Tarım İşçileri, Çocuklar, Tarım Aracıları ve Bahçe Sahipleri Temel Araştırması, Ankara, Kalkınma Atölyesi.

Development Workshop (2016), *Poverty, Rivalry and Antagonism: The Report on The Present Situation of Foreign Migrant Workers in Seasonal Agricultural Production in Turkey*, Ankara: Development Workshop Cooperative.

Development Workshop (2018), *A Child's Work Makes a Day's Wage… Agricultural Intermediaries and Child Labour in Agricultural Production in Turkey*, Ankara: Development Workshop Cooperative.

Directorate General of Migration Management-DGMM (2020), 'Statistics on Temporary Protection'. Available online: https://en.goc.gov.tr/temporary-protection27 (accessed May 2020).

Dixon, J. (2007), 'Supermarkets as New Food Authorities', in D. Burch and G. Lawrence (eds), *Supermarkets and Agri-Food Supply Chains. Transformations in the Production and Consumption of Foods*, 29–50, Cheltenham: Edward Elgar.

Dolan, C. S. (2005), 'Benevolent Intent? The Development Encounter in Kenya's Horticulture Industry', *Journal of Asian and African Studies*, 40 (6, Winter): 411–37.

Donato, K. M., D. Gabaccia, J. Holdaway, M. Manalansan IV and P. R. Pessar (2006), 'A Glass Half Full? Gender in Migration Studies', *International Migration Review*, 40 (1): 3–26.

Elson, D. and R. Pearson (1981), 'Nimble Fingers Make Cheap Workers: An Analysis of Women's Employment in Third World Export Manufacturing', *Feminist Review*, 7 (Spring): 87–107.

Elson, D. (1999), 'Labor Markets as Gendered Institutions: Equality, Efficiency and Empowerment Issues', *World Development*, 27 (3): 611–27.

Erdoğan, M. M. (2015), *Türkiye'deki Suriyeliler: Toplumsal Kabul ve Uyum*, İstanbul: Bilgi Yayınları.

Erdoğan, M. M. (2018), *Suriyeliler Barometresi: Suriyelilerle Uyum İçinde Yaşamın Çerçevesi*, İstanbul: İstanbul Bilgi Üniversitesi Yayınları.

Ertürk, Y. (2006), 'Turkey's Modern Paradoxes in Identity Politics, Women's Agency and Universal Norms', in M. Ferree and A. Tripp (eds), *Global Feminism: Transnational Women's Activism, Organizing, and, Human Rights*, 79–109, New York: New York University Press.

Espiritu, Y. L. (2005), 'Gender, Migration, and Work: Filipina Health Care Professionals to The United States', *Revue Européenne des Digrations Internationals*, 21 (1): 55–75.

Ettlinger, N. (2007), 'Precarity Unbound', *Alternatives*, 32: 319–40.

European Parliament (2016), 'Labour Market Integration of Refugees: Strategies and Good Practices, Directorate General for Internal Policies, Policy Department A. Economic and Scientific Policy'. Available online: www.europarl.europa.eu/Re gData/etudes/STUD/2016/578956/IPOL_STU(2016)578956_EN.pdf (accessed on 19 November 2019).

Fantasia, R. (1988), *Cultures of Solidarity: Consciousness, Action and Contemporary American Workers*, Berkeley and London: University of California Press.

Fantone, L. (2007), 'Precarious Changes: Gender and Generational Politics in Contemporary Italy', *Feminist Review*, 87: 5–20.

FAO (2018), Biodiversity of Turkey Contribution of Genetic Resources To Sustainable Agriculture and Food Systems, Ankara: FAO. Available online: http://www.fao.org /3/CA1517EN/ca1517en.pdf

Federici, S. (2004), *Caliban and The Witch: Women, The Body and Primitive Sccumulation*, Brooklyn, NY: Autonomedia.

Federici, S. (2008), 'Precarious Labor: A Feminist Viewpoint'. Available online: https ://inthemiddleofthewhirlwind.wordpress.com/precarious-labor-a-feminist-view point/ (accessed on 21 November 2020).

Federici, S. (2012), *Revolution at Point Zero: Housework, Reproduction, and Feminist Struggle*, Brooklyn, NY: PM Press.

FLA (2017), 'Hazelnut Workers in Turkey: Demographic Profiling; Düzce, Ordu and Sakarya', 2016. Available online: https://www.fairlabor.org/sites/default/files/docu ments/reports/demographic_profiling_hazelnut_workers_in_turkey_september _2017.pdf (accessed on 18 November 2019).

Freedman, J. (2015), *Gendering the International Asylum and Refugee Debate*, New York: Palgrave Macmillan.

Gavanas, An. and C. Calzada (2016), 'Multiplex Migration and Aspects of Precarization: Swedish Retirement Migrants to Spain and Their Service Providers', *Critical Sociology*, 42 (7): 1003–16.

Giulietti, C. (2014), 'The Welfare magnet Hypothesis and the Welfare Take-up of Migrants', *IZA World of Labour*, https://wol.iza.org/articles/welfare-magnet-hypothesis-and-welfare-take-up-of-migrants/long (accessed on 24 May 2020).

Gluck, S. B. and D. Patai (1991), *Women's Words: The Feminist Practice of Oral History*, New York: Routledge.

GNAT (TBMM) (2015), Mevsimlik Tarım İşçilerinin Sorunlarının Araştırılarak Alınması Gereken Önlemlerin Belirlenmesi Amacıyla Kurulan Meclis Araştırma Komisyonu Raporu, Sıra: 716. Available online: www.tbmm.gov.tr/sirasayi/donem24/yil01/ss.716.pdf (accessed on 12 December 2019).

Goldring, L. and P. Landolt (2011), 'Caught in the Work–Citizenship Matrix: The Lasting Effects of Precarious Legal Status on Work for Toronto Immigrants', *Globalizations*, 8 (3): 325–41.

Hardt, M. and A. Negri (2004), *Multitude: War and Democracy in The Age of Empire*, New York: Penguin Press.

Harriss-White, B. (2010), 'Work and Wellbeing in Informal Economies: The Regulative Roles of Institutions of Identity and the State', *World Development*, 38 (2): 170–83.

Hartman, T. (2008), 'States, Markets, and Other Unexceptional Communities: Informal Romanian Labour in A Spanish Agricultural Zone', *Journal of the Royal Anthropological Institute*, 14 (3): 496–514.

Harvey, D. (1982). *The Limits to Capital*, Oxford: Blackwell.

Heintz, J. (2006), 'Globalization, Economic Policy and Employment: Poverty and Gender Dimensions', Employment Strategy Papers 2006/3, Employment Policy Unit, International Labour Organization, Geneva.

Hennebry, J. (2014), 'Transnational Precarity: Women's Migration Work and Mexican Seasonal Agricultural Migration to Canada', Thematic Issue on 'Gender and Migration in The Global Economy', *International Journal of Sociology*, 44 (3): 42–59.

Hess, S. (2006), 'The Demand for Seasonal Farm Labor From Central and Eastern European Countries in German Agriculture', *E-Journal* 8, Manuscript MES 05 003 https://ecommons.cornell.edu/bitstream/handle/1813/10581/MES%2005%20003%20Hess%20final%2029April2006.pdf?sequence=1&isAllowed=y (accessed on 20 December 2019).

Hodge, P. (2015), 'A Grievable Life? The Criminalisation and Securing of Asylum Seeker Bodies in the 'Violent Frames' of Australia's Operation Sovereign Borders', *Geoforum*, 58: 122–31.

Hürriyet (2012), 'Erdoğan'dan Önemli Mesajlar', *Hürriyet Gazetesi*, 5 September. Available online: https://www.hurriyet.com.tr/gundem/erdogandan-onemli-mesajlar-21386210 (accessed April 2020).

ILO Ankara Office (2020), 'Syrians in the Turkish Labour Market'. Available online: https://www.ilo.org/wcmsp5/groups/public/---europe/---ro-geneva/-iloankara/documents/genericdocument/wcms_738618.pdf (accessed on 11 February 2020).

International Organization for Migration (IOM) (2019), 'Glossary on Migration', IML Series No. 34. Available online: https://www.iom.int/whoisamigrant#:~:text=IOM%20Definition%20of%20%E2%80%9CMigrant%E2%80%9D,for%20a%20vaiety%20of%20reasons. (accessed on 9 January 2020)

Jordan, B. and P. Brown (2007), 'Migration and Work in the United Kingdom: Mobility and the Social Order', *Mobilities*, 2 (2): 255–76.

Jørgensen, M. B. (2016), 'Precariat – What It Is and Isn't – Towards an Understanding of What It Does', *Critical Sociology*, 42 (7–8): 959–74.

Kara, S. (2012), *Bonded Labor: Tackling the System of Slavery in South Asia*, New York: Columbia University Press, ISBN 9780231158480.

Kasaba, R. (1993), *Osmanlı İmparatorluğu ve Dünya Ekonomisi*, Belge, Istanbul, ISBN 941-451-512.

Kaya, A. and A. Kıraç (2016), 'Vulnerability Assessment of Syrian Refugees in Istanbul', Support to Life, April. Available online: http://openaccess.bilgi.edu.tr:8080/xmlui/bitstream/handle/11411/823/Vulnerability%20assessment%0of%20Syrian%20refugees%20in%20%20stanbul%20April%202016.pdf?sequence¼1 (accessed on 8 April 2020).

Kaymaz, T. and O. Kadkoy (2016), 'Syrians in Turkey—The Economics of Integration', ALSHARQ Forum Expert Brief.

KEİG (2015), 'Kadın Emeği ve Istihdamına Ilişkin Bilgi Notları', KEİG Platformu, İstanbul, Available online: http://www.keig.org/content/kitapcik/.bilgi%20notlari%20Agustos%202015.pdf (accessed on 10 October 2019).

Keyder, Ç. and Z. Yenal (2011), 'Agrarian Change Under Globalization: Markets and Insecurity in Turkish Agriculture', *Journal of Agrarian Change*, 11 (1): 60–86.

Keyder, Ç. and Z. Yenal (2013), *Bildiğimiz Tarımın Sonu Küresel Iktidar ve Köylülük*, İstanbul: İletişim Yayınları.

Knapp, Gudrun-Axeli (2005), 'Race, Class, Gender: Reclaiming Baggage in Fast Traveling Theories', *European Journal of Women's Studies*, 12 (3): 249–65.

Koettl, J. (2009), *Human Trafficking, Modern Day Slavery and Economic Exploitation*, (Social Protection Discussion Paper No. 0911), Washington, DC: World Bank.

Kofman, E., A. Phizacklea, P. Raghuram and R. Sales (2000), *Gender and International Migration in Europe: Employment, Welfare and Politics*, London and New York: Routledge.

Kusadokoro, M., T. Maru and U. Gültekin (2016), 'Network and Intermediaries in Seasonal Agricultural Labour Markets in Turkey', *International Journal of Food and Agricultural Economics*, 4 (2): 51–67.

Kutlu, Z. (2015), From the Ante-Chamber to The Living Room: A Brief Assessment on NGO's Doing Work for Syrian Refugees, Istanbul: Anadolu Kultur and Acik Toplum Vakfi (Open Society Foundation).

Lewis, H, P. Dwyer, S. Hodkinson and L. Waite (2015), *Precarious Lives: Forced Labour, Exploitation and Asylum*, Bristol: Policy Press.

Ludvig, A. (2006), 'Differences Between Women? Intersecting Voices in a Female Narrative', *European Journal of Women's Studies*, 13 (3): 245–58.

Lummis, T. (1987), *Listening to History: The Authenticity of Oral Evidence*, London: Hutchinson Education.

Maher, S. (2009), *False Promises: Migrant Workers in The Global Garment Industry* (Clean Clothes Campaign Discussion Paper), Amsterdam: Clean Clothes Campaign.

Makal, A. (2012), 'Türkiye'de Kadın Emeğinin Tarihsel Kökenleri: 1920–1960', in A. Makal and G. Toksöz (eds), *Geçmişten Günümüze Türkiye'de Kadın Emeği*, 44–61, Ankara: İmge Yayınevi.

Martin, P. L. (2016), *Migrant Workers in Commercial Agriculture*, Geneva: ILO. Available online: www.ilo.org/wcmsp5/groups/public/ed_protect/protrav/migrant/documents/publication/wcms_538710.pdf

Massey, D. S., J. Arango, G. Hugo, A. Kouaouci, A. Pellegrino and J. E. Taylor (1998), *Worlds in Motion: Understanding International Migration at the End of the Millennium*, Oxford: Clarendon Press.

McKay, F. H., S. L. Thomas and S. Kneebone (2012), 'It Would Be Okay If They Came Through the Proper Channels: Community Perceptions and Attitudes Toward Asylum Seekers in Australia', *Journal of Refugee Studies*, 25 (1): 113–33.

McMichael, P. and H. Friedmann (2007), 'Situating the Retailing Revolution', in D. Burch and G. Lawrence (eds), *Supermarkets and Agri-Food Supply Chains. Transformations in The Production and Consumption of Foods*, 291–319, Cheltenham: Edward Elgar.

Metso, M. and N. Le Feuvre (2006), 'Quantitative Methods for Analysing Gender, Ethnicity and Migration' (York: University of York). Available online: http://www.york.ac.uk/res/researchintegration/Integrative_Research_Methods/Metso%20and%20Le%20Feuvre%20Quantitative%20Methods%20April%202007.pdfESSE (accessed on 09 March 2020).

MEVSİMLİK İŞÇİ GÖÇÜ İLETİŞİM AĞI (MIGA) (2012), *Tarımda Mevsimlik Işçi Göçü Türkiye Durum Özeti*, Istanbul: Friedrich Ebert Stiftung.

Mezzadra, S. and B. Neilson (2013), *Border as Method, or, the Multiplication of Labor*, Durham, NC and London: Duke University Press.

Mezzadri, A. (2020), 'The Informal Labours of Social Reproduction', *Global Labour Journal*, 11 (2): 156–63.

Mies, M. (1982), *The Lace Makers of Nasapur: Indian Housewives Produce for the World Market*, London: Zed Press.

Mies, M. (1986), *Patriarchy and Accumulation on a World Scale: Women in the International Division of Labour*, London: Zed.

Ministry of Family, Work and Social Services-MoFWSS (2020), 'Yabancıların çalışma izinleri', Available online: https://www.ailevecalisma.gov.tr/istatistikler/calisma-hayati-istatistikleri/resmi-istatistik-programi/yabancilarin-calisma-izinleri/ (accessed on 05 January 2020).

Morokvasic, M. (1984), 'The Overview: Birds of Passage Are Also Women', *International Migration Review*, 68 (18): 886–907.

Mura, E. (2016), 'Dynamics of Intermediation in the Agricultural Labor Market: Women Workers in Adapazarı, Turkey', PhD diss., Middle East Technical University. Ankara.

Nawa, F. (2017), 'Syrian Refugees Married Early Face Isolation and Domestic Violence', *Financial Times*, 11 October. Available online: https://www.ft.com/content/3754ce46-7204-11e7-93ff-99f383b09ff9 (accessed on 08 September 2019).

Nieto, J. M. (2014), 'Labour and Gender Relations in Moroccan Strawberry Culture', in J. Gertel and S. r. Sippel (eds), *Seasonal Workers in Mediterranean Agriculture: The Social Costs of Eating Fresh*, 217–28, London: Earthscan.

OECD (2011), 'Evaluation of Agricultural Policy Reforms in Turkey'. Available online: https://read.oecd-ilibrary.org/agriculture-and-food/evaluation-of-agricultural-policy-reforms-in-turkey_9789264113220-en#page4 (accessed on 12 July 2020).

OECD (2019), 'Average Usual Weekly Hours Worked on the Main Job'. Available online: https://stats.oecd.org/Index.aspx?lang=en&SubSessionId=b0ce6517-1890-4d43-bb5bc7f4faf814eb&themetreeid=13 (accessed on 1 December 2020).

Özbek, A. (2007), 'New Actors of New Poverty: The "Other" Children of Çukurova', MA diss., Middle East Technical University, Ankara.

Özer, M. H. (2014), 'The Effects of The Marshall Plan Aids to The Development of The Agricultural Sector in Turkey, The 1948–1953 Period', *International Journal of Economics and Financial Issues*, 4 (2): 427–39.

Pamuk, Ş. (2009), 'Agriculture and Economic Development in Turkey, 1870–2000', in P. Lains and V. Pinilla (eds), *Agriculture and Economic Development in Europe Since 1870*, 375–96, London and New York: Routledge.

Papadopoulos, A. (2015), 'In What Way Is Greek Family Farming Defying the Economic Crisis?', *Agriregionieuropa*, 11 (43), unpaginated. https://agriregionieuropa.univpm.it/it/content/article/31/43/what-way-greek-family-farming-defying-economic-crisis (accessed on 14 November 2020).

Peck, J. (1996), *Work-place: The Social Regulation of Labor Markets*, New York: Guilford.

Pelek, D. (2010), 'Seasonal Migrant in Agriculture: The Cases of Ordu and Polatlı', MA diss., Boğaziçi University, Istanbul.

Pelek, D. (2019), 'Syrian Refugees as Seasonal Migrant Workers: Re-Construction of Unequal Power Relations in Turkish Agriculture', *Journal of Refugee Studies*, 32 (4): 605–29.

Peri, G. (2014), 'Do Immigrant Workers Depress the Wages of Native Workers?', *IZA World of Labour*, https://wol.iza.org/uploads/articles/42/pdfs/do-immigrant-workers-depress-the-wages-of-native-workers.pdf (accessed on 24 May 2020).

Peschner, J. and P. Tanay (2017), 'Labour Market Performance of Refugees in the EU', European Commission Directorate-General for Employment, Social Affairs and Inclusion Unit, Working Paper 1/2017: Analytical Support to the Employment and Social Developments in Europe 2016 Review (ESDE 2016) Chapter 3: The Labour Market and Social Integration of Refugees in the EU.

Pessar, P. R. (1984), 'The Linkage Between the Household and Workplace in The Experience of Dominican Immigrant Women in The United States', *International Migration Review*, 18 (4): 1188–211.

Pessar, P. (1986), 'The Role of Gender in Dominican Settlement Patterns in the United States', in J. Nash and H. Safa (eds), *Women and Change in Latin America*, 273–94, South Hadley: Bergin & Garvey Publishers.

Phizacklea, A., ed. (1983), *One Way Ticket: Migration and Female Labour*, London: Routledge and Kegan Paul.

Ploeg, J. D. van der (2008), *The New Peasantries. Struggles for Autonomy and Sustainability in an Era of Empire and Globalization*, London: Earthscan.

Polanyi, K. (2001), *The Great Transformation: The Political and Economic Origins of Our Time*, 2nd edn, Boston: Beacon Press.

Pollard, D. (2006), 'The Gangmaster System in The UK – The Perspective of A Trade Unionist', in S. Barrientos and C. Dolan (eds), *Ethical Sourcing in the Global Food System*, 115–28, London: Earthscan.

Portes, A. and S. Sassen-Koob (1987), 'Making It Underground: Comparative Material on The Informal Sector in Western Market Economies', *American Journal of Sociology*, 93 (1): 30–61.

Potot, S. (2008), 'Strategies of Visibility and Invisibility: Rumanians and Moroccans in El Ejido, Spain', in S. Jansen and S. Löfving (eds), *Struggles for Home: Violence, Hope and the Movement of People*, 109–28, Oxford and New York: Berghahn.

Preibisch, K. and E. Encalada Grez (2010), 'The Other Side of El Otro Lado: Mexican Migrant Women and Labor Flexibility in Canadian Agriculture', *Signs*, 35 (2): 289–316.

Richards, C., H. Bjørkhaug, G. Lawrence and G. Hickman (2013), 'Retailer-driven Agricultural Restructuring – Australia, the UK and Norway in Comparison', *Agriculture and Human Values*, 30: 235–45.

Robinson, A. (2011), 'The Precariat and the Cuts: Reconstructing Autonomy. Andy Robinson Theory', Blog 2, 20 April. Available online: http://andyrobinsontheory blog2.blogspot.dk/ (accessed on 2 May 2021).

Rogaly, B. (1996), 'Agricultural Growth and The Structure Of "Casual" Labor-Hiring in Rural West Bengal', *Journal of Peasant Studies*, 23 (4): 141–65.

Sassen, S. (2000), 'Women's Burden: Counter-geographies of Globalization and the Feminization of Survival', *Journal of International Affairs*, 53 (2): 503–24.

Sassen, S. (2014), *Expulsions: Brutality and Complexity in The Global Economy*, Harvard University Press.

Schierup, C, A. Ålund and B. Likić-Brborić (2014), 'Migration, Precarization and the Democratic Deficit in Global Governance', *International Migration*, 53 (3): 50–63.

Schierup, C, R. Munck, B. Likic-Brboric and A. Neergaard (2015), *Migration, Precarity, and Global Governance: Challenges and Opportunities for Labour*, Oxford: Oxford University Press.

Schierup, C. and M. B. Jørgensen (2016), 'From "Social Exclusion" to "Precarity. The Becoming-Migrant of Labour: An Introduction"', in M. B. Jørgensen and C. Schierup (eds), *Politics of Precarity: Migrant Conditions, Struggles and Experiences*, 1–29, Leiden and Boston, Brill, Studies in Critical Social Sciences.

Schrover, M. and D. M. Moloney (2013), *Gender, Migration and Categorisation: Making Distinctions Between Migrants in Western Countries, 1945–2010*, Amsterdam: Amsterdam University Press.

Semerci, P. U. and E. Erdoğan (2017), *Ben Kendim Büyüdüm Demiyorum: Adana'da (Mevsimlik Gezici) Tarım Işçilerinin Çocuklarının Yaşam Koşullarının Çocuğun Iyi Olma Hali Perspektifinden Iyileştirilmesi Projesi Araştırma Sonuçları*, Istanbul: Istanbul Bilgi University.

Sharma, N. (2006), *Home Economics: Nationalism and The Making of' Migrant Workers' in Canada*, Toronto: University of Toronto Press.

Silver, B. J. (2003), *Forces of Labor: Workers' Movements and Globalization since 1870*, Cambridge: Cambridge University Press.

Support to Life (Hayata Destek Derneği) (2014), 'Mevsimlik Gezici Tarım İşçiliği Araştırma Raporu'. Available online: http://hayatadestek.org/yayinlarimiz/Mev simlik_Gezici_Tarım_İsciligi_%202014_Arastırma_Raporu.pdf (accessed on 11 November 2019).

Support to Life [Hayata Destek Derneği] (2016), 'Vulnerability Assessment of Syrian Refugees in İstanbul'. Available online: https://data2.unhcr.org/ar/documents/dow nload/54518 (accessed on 09 March 2020).

Svensson, M., R. Urinboyev, A. W. Svensson, P. Lundqvist, M. Littorin and M. Albin (2013), 'Migrant Agricultural Workers and Their Socio-Economic, Occupational and Health Conditions: A Literature Review'. Available online: ssrn.com/abstract =2297559 or dx.doi.org/10.2139/ssrn.2297559 (accessed on 10 October 2019).

Şimşek, D. (2018), 'Integration Processes of Syrian Refugees in Turkey: "Class-based Integration"', *Journal of Refugee Studies*, 33 (3): 537–54.

Tschöll, C. (2014), 'Precarity: Causes, Effects and Consequences of Insecure Working and Living Conditions in A Multicultural, Rural Area of Northern Italy (South Tyrol)', *Journal of Education Culture and Society*, 2: 82–90.

Tsianos, V. and D. Papadopoulos (2006), 'Precarity: A Savage Journey to The Heart of Embodied Capitalism'. Available online: https://transversal.at/transversal/1106/tsianos-papadopoulos/en (accessed on 15 August 2020).

Ulukan, N. C. and U. Ulukan (2011), 'Kriz ve Göç: Türkiye Gürcistan Arası Nüfus Hareketleri Üzerinden Bir Tartışma', in E. Akbostancı and O. Erdoğdu (eds), *Küresel Bunalım ve Karadeniz Bölgesi Ekonomileri*, 119–32, Türkiye Ekonomi Kurumu, Ankara: İmaj Yayınları.

UNHCR (2020), 'Figures at a Glance'. Available online: https://www.unhcr.org/tr/en/figures-at-a-glance#:~:text=An%20unprecedented%2079.5%20million%20people,under%20the%20age%20of%2018 (accessed on 9 August 2020).

UNWOMEN-ASAM (2018), *Needs Assessment of Syrian Women and Girls Under Temporary Protection Status in Turkey*, Ankara: ASAM.

Vaupel, S. and P. L. Martin (1986), 'Activity and Regulation of Farm Labor Contractors', Giannini Foundation Information Series No. 86-3, https://s.giannini.ucop.edu/uploads/giannini_public/c8/2f/c82fed18-eded-484d-a346-d36847bd957e/863-contractors.pdf (accessed on 14 December 2019).

Verité Fair Labour Worldwide (2005), 'Protecting Overseas Workers: Research Findings and Strategic Perspectives on Labor Protections for Foreign Contract Workers in Asia And the Middle East', New York. Available online: https://www.verite.org/wp-content/uploads/2016/11/Protecting-Overseas-Workers.pdf (accessed on 2 January 2021).

Vosko, L. F. (2010), *Managing the Margins: Gender, Citizenship, And the International Regulation of Precarious Employment*, Oxford: Oxford University Press.

Waite, L. (2009), 'A Place and Space for a Critical Geography of Precarity?', *Geography Compass*, 3 (1): 412–33.

Walby, S. (2007), 'Complexity Theory, Systems Theory, and Multiple Intersecting Social Inequalities', *Philosophy of the Social Sciences*, 37 (4): 449–70.

Weeks, K. (2011), *The Problem with Work: Feminism, Marxism, Antiwork Politics and Postwork Imaginaries*, Durham: Duke University Press.

Wilford, R. and R. Miller (1998), *Women, Ethnicity and Nationalism*, London: Routledge.

Yıldırım, U. D. (2014), '1980 Sonrası Türkiye Tarımında Yapısal Dönüşüm ve Mevsimlik Tarım İşçileri', PhD diss., Istanbul University, Istanbul.

Zetter, R., H. Ruaudel and K. Schuettler (2017), *Refugees' Right to Work and Access to Labor Markets, KNOMAD Study*, Washington, DC: World Bank.

Index

absorption strategies 4, 137
Adana 9, 36, 39–40, 42, 50, 55–6, 59–62, 67–8, 70–2, 76–7, 80, 82, 93–4, 98–9, 105–6, 108, 110, 112–13, 115, 119–20, 122–3, 126, 128–9, 145, 147
Adıyaman 38, 61, 124
agency of refugees 5
agribusiness commodity chains 31
agricultural sale cooperatives 34
agricultural sector 42, 46, 65–6, 68, 84, 88, 90, 101, 108, 115, 133–6, 138–42, 146
agri-food supply chains 31
antagonism 59
antagonistic confrontations 5
apricots 29, 36, 125
Arabic 9, 109, 129–30
artificialization 30, 34
asylum seekers 2, 22, 54–5, 60, 68
Azerbaijan 39, 44–6
Azerbaijanis 9, 36, 42, 44

biographies 8
bonded labour 1, 6–12, 15, 25–8, 103–4, 126, 131, 141–2
Bursa 4, 35, 50, 55–6

cash crops 33, 36–7
casual jobs 4, 58
children 1–2, 4, 6, 12, 15–16, 22, 25, 28, 36, 40–1, 50–1, 53, 56–7, 60, 65–6, 69–70, 73–4, 76–9, 82–98, 100–1, 111, 115, 117, 119, 122–3, 125–30, 133–4, 136–7, 139–40, 148
citizenship 10, 18, 32, 49, 52, 62, 136
citrus fruits 36, 86
civil marriages 81
class 5–6, 16, 18, 24–6, 50, 58, 83, 97–8, 140
classes of labour 26
coffeehouse 44

commercialization 30
commoditization 30
confinement 123, 126, 131, 142
context-dependent 2, 19, 134–5
contingent work 16
cotton 9, 34–6, 42, 78, 86, 94–6, 117–18, 148
Çukurova Plantation 35
cultures of solidarity 11

daily wage (yevmiye) 41, 58–9, 93–4, 115–16, 120, 136
dayıbaşı 1, 10, 41, 68–9, 74, 107, 126–7
debt bondage 25, 27, 106
defamilization 31
dependents 22
deportable 32
Development Workshop 11, 37, 40, 42, 61, 70, 72, 77, 86–8, 94, 99, 108, 112–13, 121, 125, 127–8, 145
differential inclusion 3–4, 26, 31, 49, 70, 133–4, 140
Dilucu border 45
discrimination 31–3
domestic labour force 9
domestic servitude 7
double movement 5, 15, 140, 145

Egypt 30, 106, 147
elçi 10, 107
Emergency Social Safety Net-Kızılay card 53
ethnicity 3, 5, 24–5, 50, 133–4, 140

family members 7, 36, 73, 76, 107, 111, 117, 119, 126, 138–9, 147
family registry booklet 81
feminist methodology 7
feminization 6, 11, 13, 16, 19–21, 41, 68, 138
feminization of precarity 16, 19

fertilizers 30
flexibilization 19–20
food authorities 31
forced migration 7, 39, 54, 63, 69
formal education 51, 56, 63, 137
free and unfree labour 26

Gaziantep 4, 50, 55–6
gender 3, 5–7, 9, 11–13, 16, 18, 20–2, 24–6, 28, 32, 50–1, 56, 66–7, 74–6, 80, 82–4, 97, 101, 116, 133–4, 138, 140, 148
Georgia 39, 43, 46, 135
Georgians 9, 11, 29, 36, 42–4, 147
global capitalism 5, 17, 27, 75
global disorder 17

hazelnuts 9, 29, 36, 42–4, 86–7, 115–16
health-care services 53
hegemonic discourses 24
high-value crops 35
home-based work 20
humanitarian assistance 18, 49, 136
human trafficking 7
hyper-precarity 2

ıcar 35
illegalization 18
imece 35
income-generating activities 63, 68, 83, 90, 138–9
in-depth interviews 8, 10, 106
informality 17, 21, 38, 107–8
informalization 6, 66
insecure 3, 16, 49, 58, 74
integration 3–5, 7–8, 10–12, 24, 27–9, 31, 49, 53–6, 58, 62, 103, 134, 136–7, 140–1
intensification 6, 23, 66, 70, 75, 83–4, 101
interconnected disadvantages 5, 25, 140
interconnectedness 6, 15, 19, 66–7
intersectionality 11, 23–4
intersectional vulnerabilities 3, 5, 9, 15–16, 25, 134, 140
irregular migrants 147
irrigated areas 30
isolation 126, 129
Istanbul 56–7
İzmir 4

Kavalali Ibrahim Pasha 35, 147
Kemal Atatürk 33
Kilis 4, 50
kimlik (ID card) 52
Kurds 29, 39, 124

labour contractors 104–6, 139
labour-intensive sectors 56, 58, 73, 85, 135
labour intermediaries 1, 3–5, 10, 12–13, 41–2, 44, 84–5, 87, 89, 91, 103, 105–9, 111–12, 114–15, 119, 122–3, 126–7, 131, 133–4, 136–7, 139–42, 145
labour regimes 17
labour segment 1
land fragmentation 30, 34
landholdings 9
Law on Foreigners and International Protection 52
legal rights 49, 62, 82, 136
life histories 8

male labour migration 7
male polygamy (*kumalık*) 81
Mardin 38–9, 46, 61, 124
market/non-market relations 21
Marshall Plan 33
masculine aura 74, 84
Mecbur 69, 71
mechanization 30, 33–4, 146
migrant precariat 2, 18
migrant women 21, 22, 75, 80, 84, 138
Morocco 30
muhtars (village heads) 115
multiplication of labour 26, 31, 70
multitude 20

Nahcivan 44
national and ethnic boundaries 21
non-material precarity 22
Norway 31

On Fertile Lands 29, 31, 33, 35, 38–9, 41, 43, 45, 47
Orhan Kemal 38

passive victims 7
patriarchal control 5, 23, 68, 73–4, 84, 134, 138–9
patriarchal hegemony 74

patriarchal relations   3, 22, 66, 74, 80, 101, 133–4
permanent crops   30
permanent workers   4
pesticides   30, 96
piece rate *(kabala)*   114, 117
poverty   23, 46, 62–3, 90, 97–9, 107, 137, 139
precariat   3, 12, 15, 17–18, 65, 79, 85, 90, 101, 124, 134, 139–40
precariousness   17–18, 22, 55
precariousness in employment   17
precarious work   2, 17, 22
precarious workers   2, 17, 135
precarity   16–20, 22–3, 30, 46, 49, 53–4, 88, 133
precarization   1–6, 11–13, 15–17, 19, 21, 23, 25, 27, 30, 35, 46, 49, 54–5, 66, 74–5, 84–5, 88, 107, 124, 133–7, 140–1
proletarianization   26

race to the bottom   15
realm of production   11, 20, 66, 131, 134, 143
realm of social reproduction   16, 19, 74, 75, 131, 136, 138, 143
Recep Tayyip Erdoğan   49
recruitment   3, 5–6, 12–13, 27, 32, 44, 46, 103, 105–6, 111–12, 114, 124, 130, 133–4, 141–3
refugee camps   3, 10, 49
Refugee Convention-1951   52, 54
refugee women   11, 66, 67, 69
Regulation on Temporary Protection (TP)   52
remuneration   3, 5, 12–13, 25, 27, 42, 103, 114, 131, 134, 141–3, 145
reproductive labour   11, 19–21, 27–8, 75, 103, 138, 143
retention   3, 5, 12–13, 27, 103, 123, 131, 133–4, 140–3
rural areas   29, 32, 96, 131, 142

salary wage system   118
Şanlıurfa   4, 38–9, 42, 61, 78, 95, 106–8, 113, 116, 118, 123–4, 145, 148
Sarp border   43
seasonal agricultural work- workers   1–5, 8, 11–13, 22–3, 25, 27, 29–30, 33, 35–8, 40–2, 46, 58–9, 61, 65–8, 73–5, 79, 85–9, 96–100, 103, 106, 110, 112, 114, 120, 122–5, 128–9, 133, 135–8, 140–1, 143, 146
semi-subsistence   34
Settlement Law of Turkey   52
sexual exploitation   7
sharecropping   115–18, 147–8
shelter conditions   124–5
small farms   30
social exclusion   32, 62
social integration   7, 11, 28
social reproduction   4, 6, 11–12, 15–16, 19–23, 65–7, 74–5, 101, 131, 134, 136, 138, 140, 143
social services   49, 52–3, 86, 136
social status   5, 25, 140
social transformations   5, 140
state economic enterprises   34
state-owned banks   34
subsistence crops   33
sugar beet   36, 72, 116–17
supply-side strategies   4, 137
Syria   2, 9–10, 19, 46, 49–52, 60, 68–9, 71, 73, 80–1, 83, 100, 126, 130, 135, 147
Syrian Barometer   51
Syrian children   57, 87–8
Syrian migrants   13, 56–8, 61, 80, 112–13
Syrian refugees   1–20, 25–6, 39–40, 49, 52, 56, 58, 62–3, 65, 68, 70, 85, 90, 100, 106–7, 109, 128, 133–7, 140, 145
Syrian women   9, 22, 65–6, 68–74, 77, 80–1, 83, 100, 138, 147
Syrians   1–4, 6, 9–13, 15, 19, 25, 36, 42–3, 49–53, 55–62, 65–8, 72, 74, 77, 80, 85, 88, 90, 92, 94, 97, 100, 109, 112–14, 116, 122, 124, 128–30, 133, 135–7, 139–40

tea harvesting   43–4
temporary migrants   3
tent settlements   5, 9, 53, 59, 67, 69, 77, 79, 87, 109, 113, 123–9, 131, 133, 136, 140–2
three Ds   31
tourist visas   39, 44, 147
transnational connectedness   5, 141
Tunisia   30

Turkey   1–15, 17, 19, 22–3, 25–7, 29–30, 33–9, 41–7, 49–60, 62–3, 65, 67–9, 71, 73–4, 78–86, 88, 90, 96, 100–1, 103, 106–9, 111–15, 119, 122–4, 126, 129–30, 133–43, 145, 147–8
Turkish economy   4, 29, 146
Turkish Republic   33

ultra-exploitation   6, 66, 136
Umayyad Mosque   49
university graduates   51
unpaid work   84, 115

vegetables   9, 30, 34, 36, 42, 109, 116, 119
vulnerable labour force   2, 4, 65, 134, 137

wage cards   119, 122
wage payment system   3, 5, 120, 133–4, 141
Western countries   3
women migrants   21
women's experiences   7–8
working permits   39
work regimes   11, 15
worst forms of child labour   85–6, 112

Printed in the USA
CPSIA information can be obtained
at www.ICGtesting.com
LVHW011624100224
771437LV00002B/202